Sunfaces

Handrawn Illustrations to Color and Design

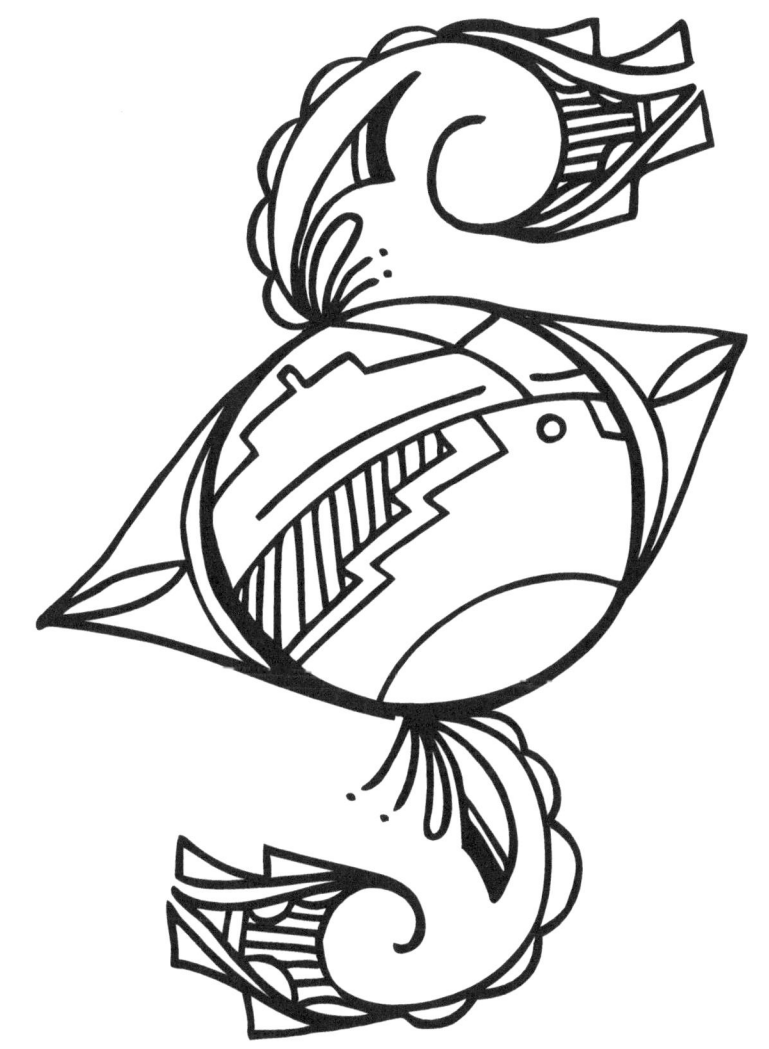

By Mallery Quetawki (Zuni Pueblo)

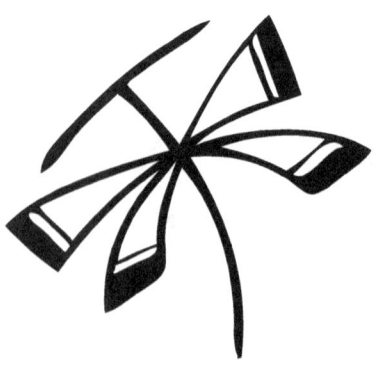

SUNFACES
HANDRAWN ILLUSTRATIONS TO COLOR AND DESIGN

ISBN-13: 978-1468018660

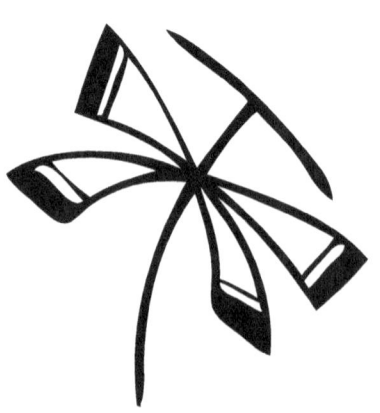

Designs are authentic Zuni in the style of artist Mallery Quetawki
www.zuniartisan.webs.com

The sun is a revered deity in most Native American cultures, including my tribe, the A:Shiwi (Zuni). We believe that the Sun Father is the creator of all life on earth. We pay homage to the Sun by symbolizing him on paintings, pottery, textiles and other cultural items and wares.

Each artist has their own representation of the Sunface. Here are a few of my own with several blank templates to design your own Sunface. The following pages can be colored with crayons, colored pencils, pens and markers. However, if using markers, place a sheet of paper behind the page you are coloring to avoid bleeding on the next page. Enjoy!

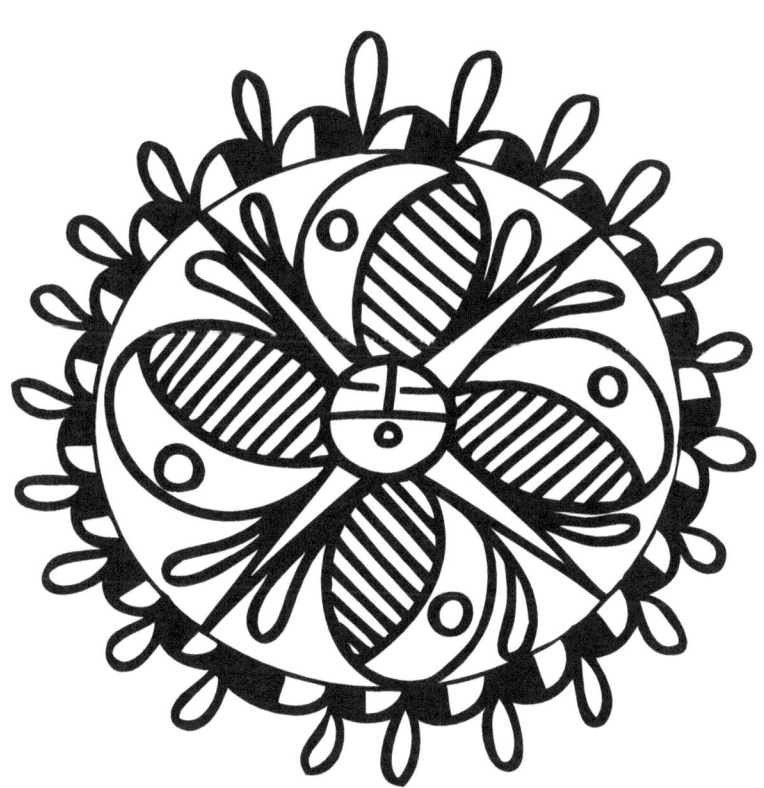

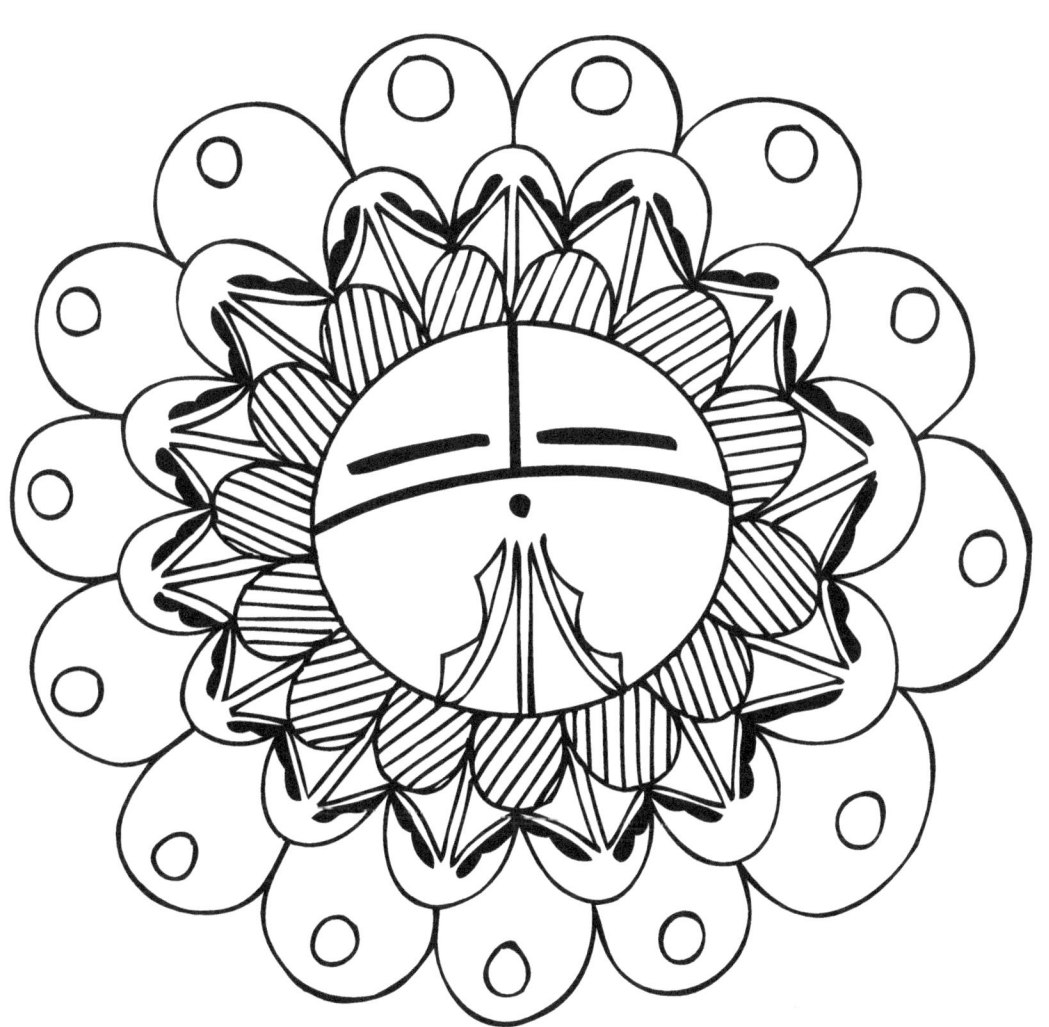

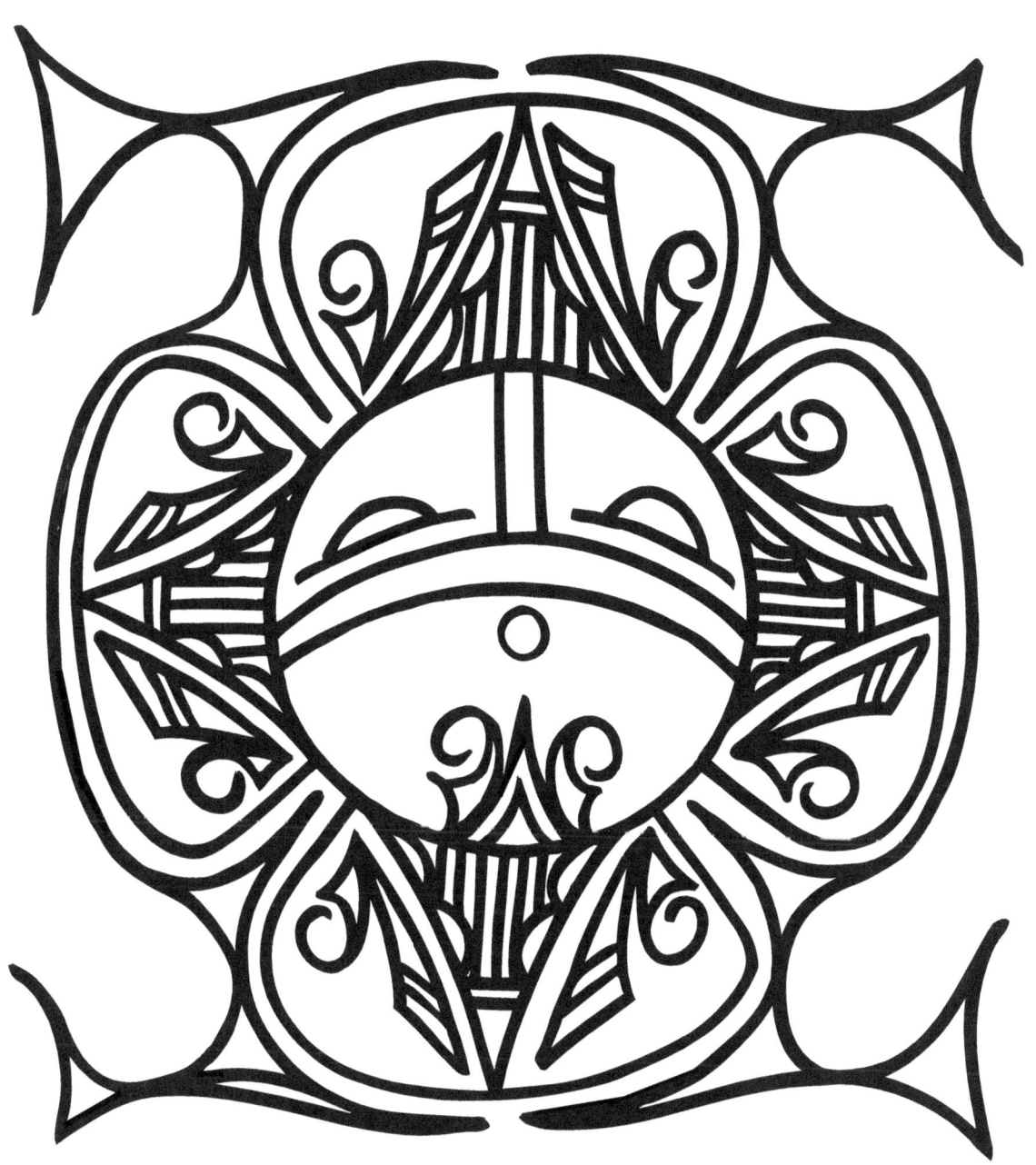

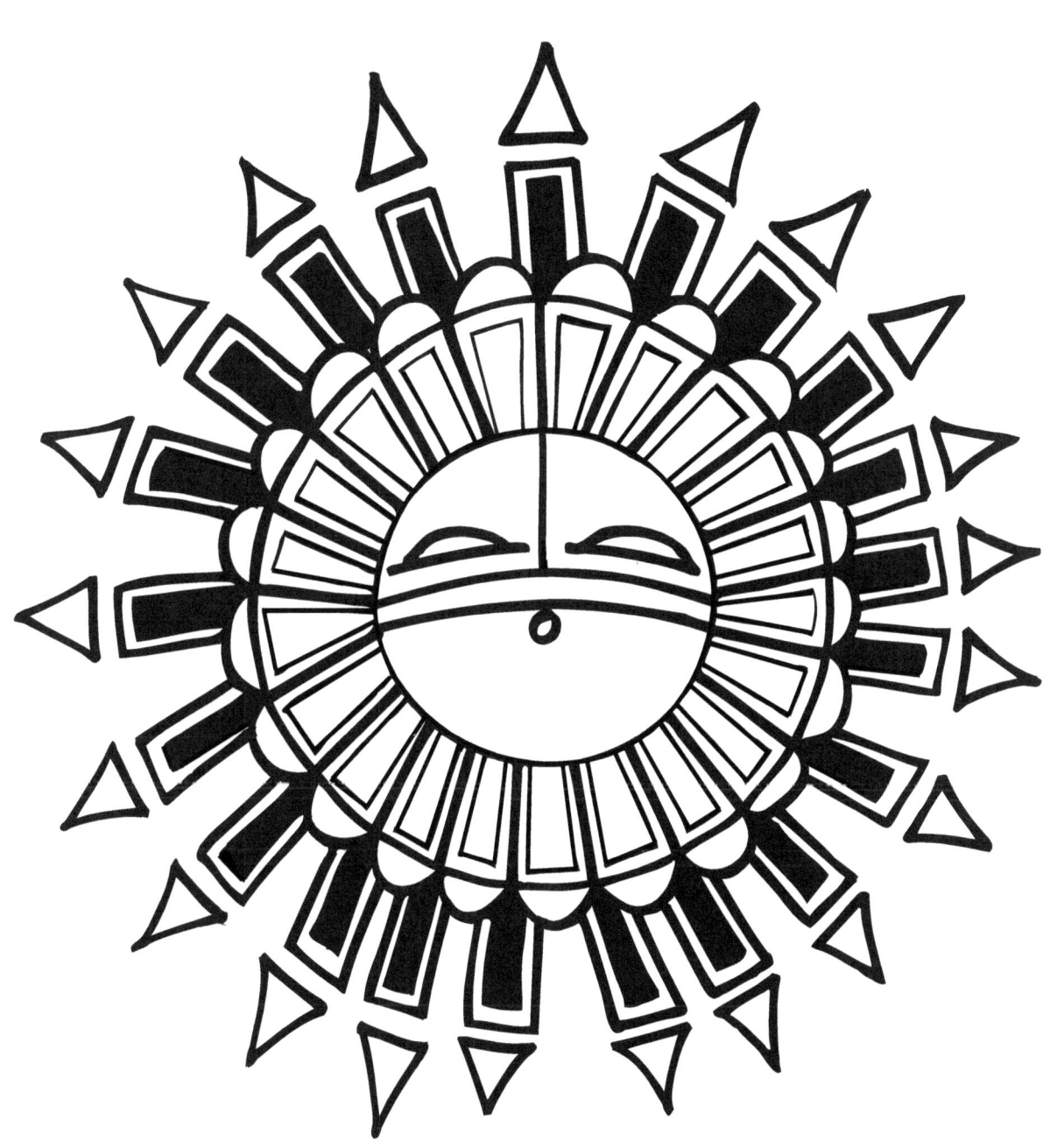

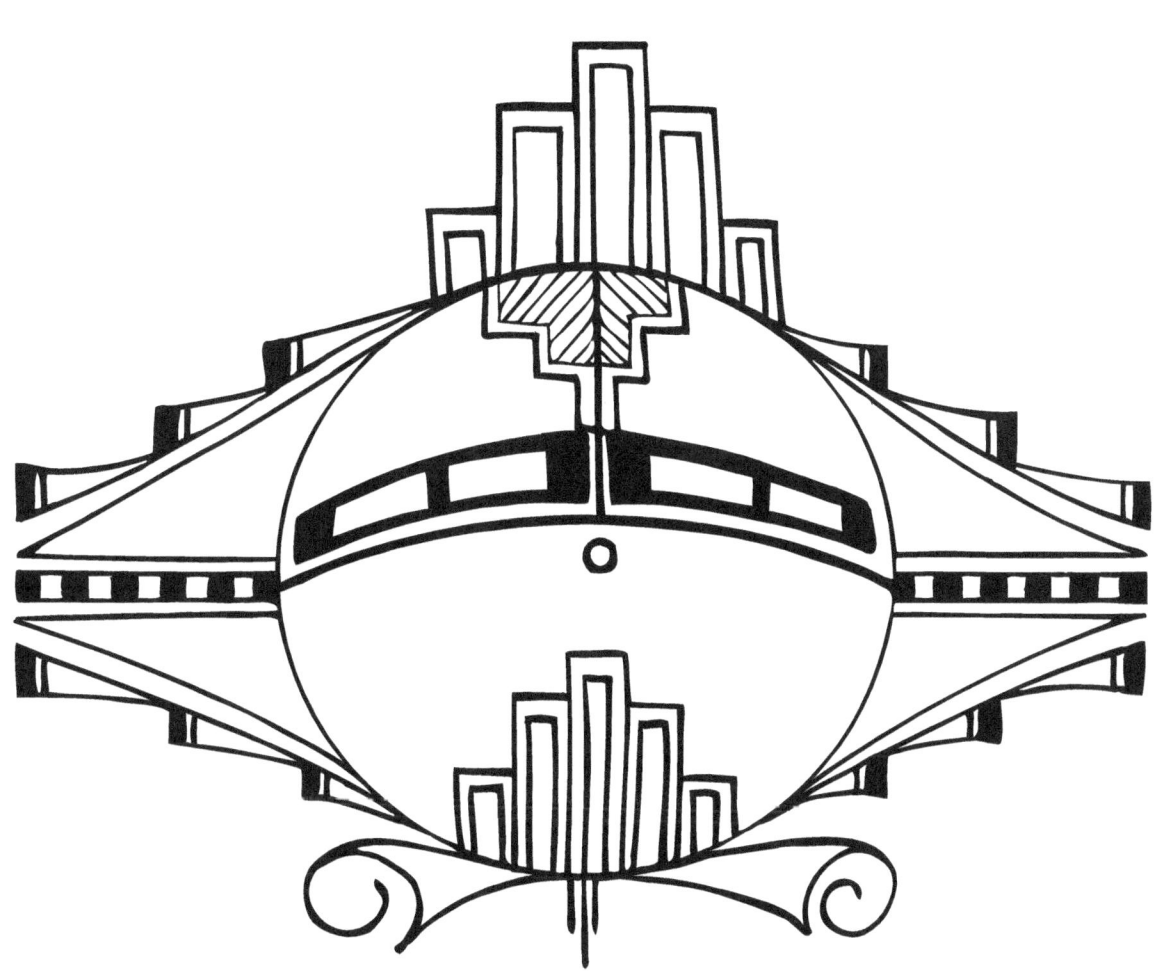

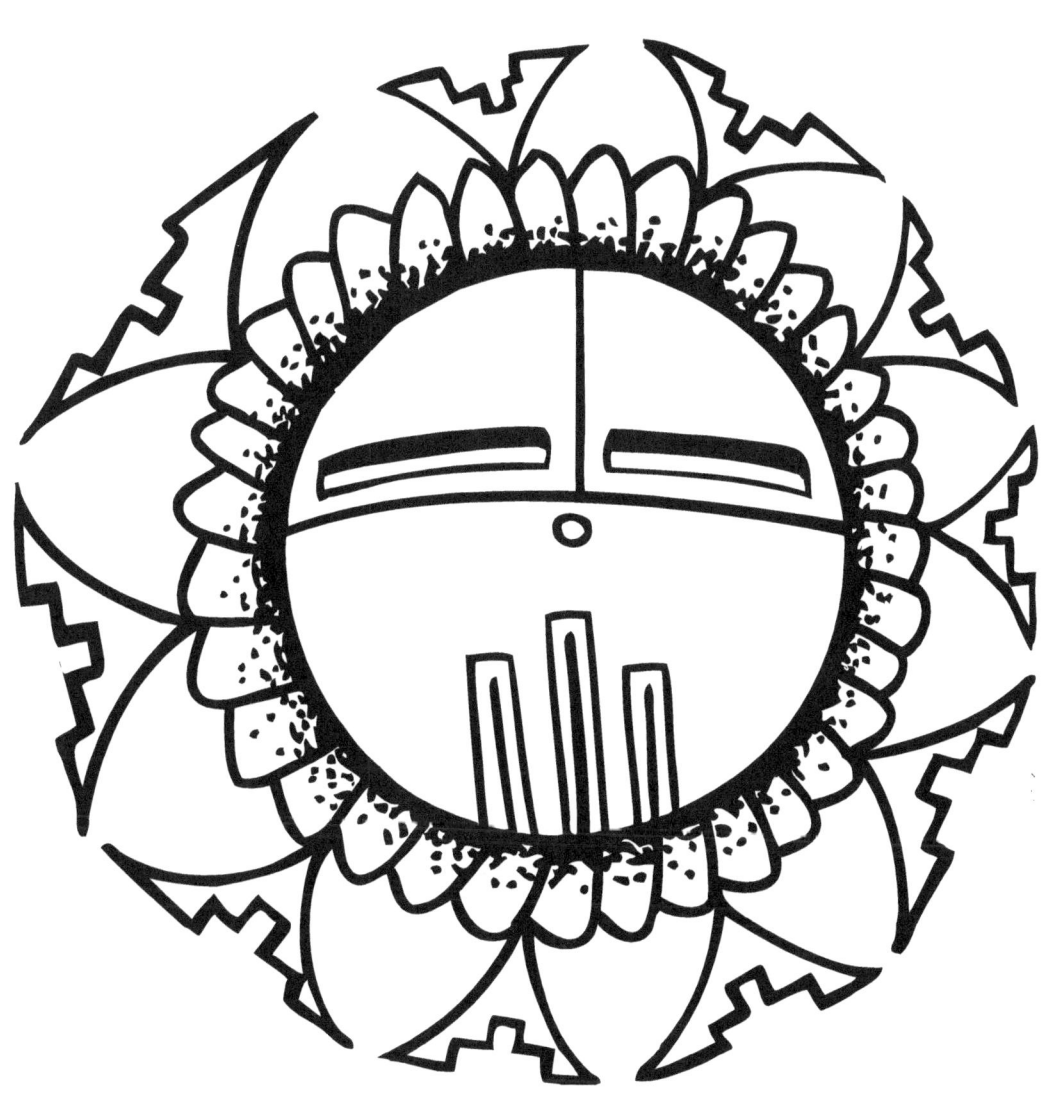

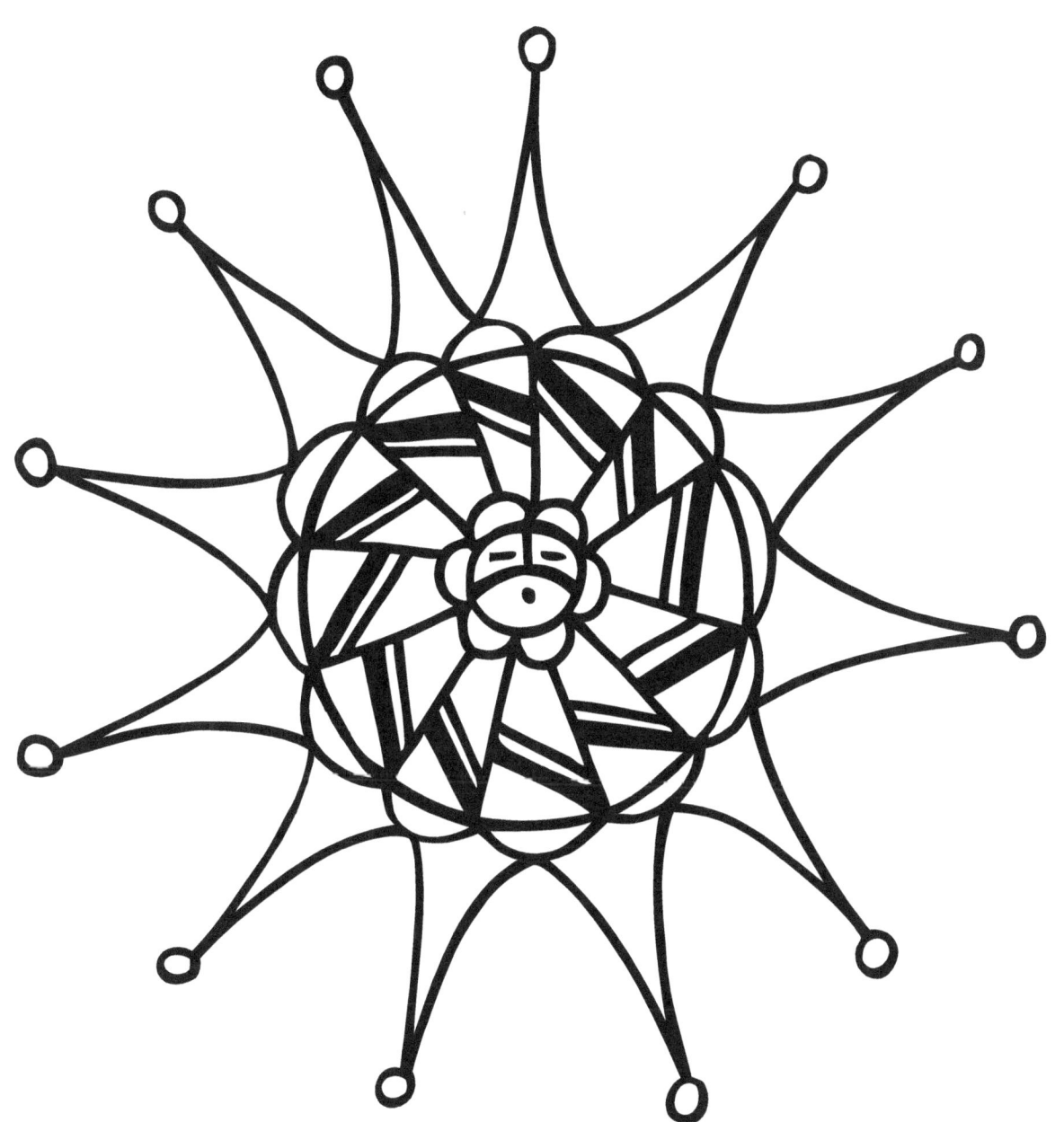

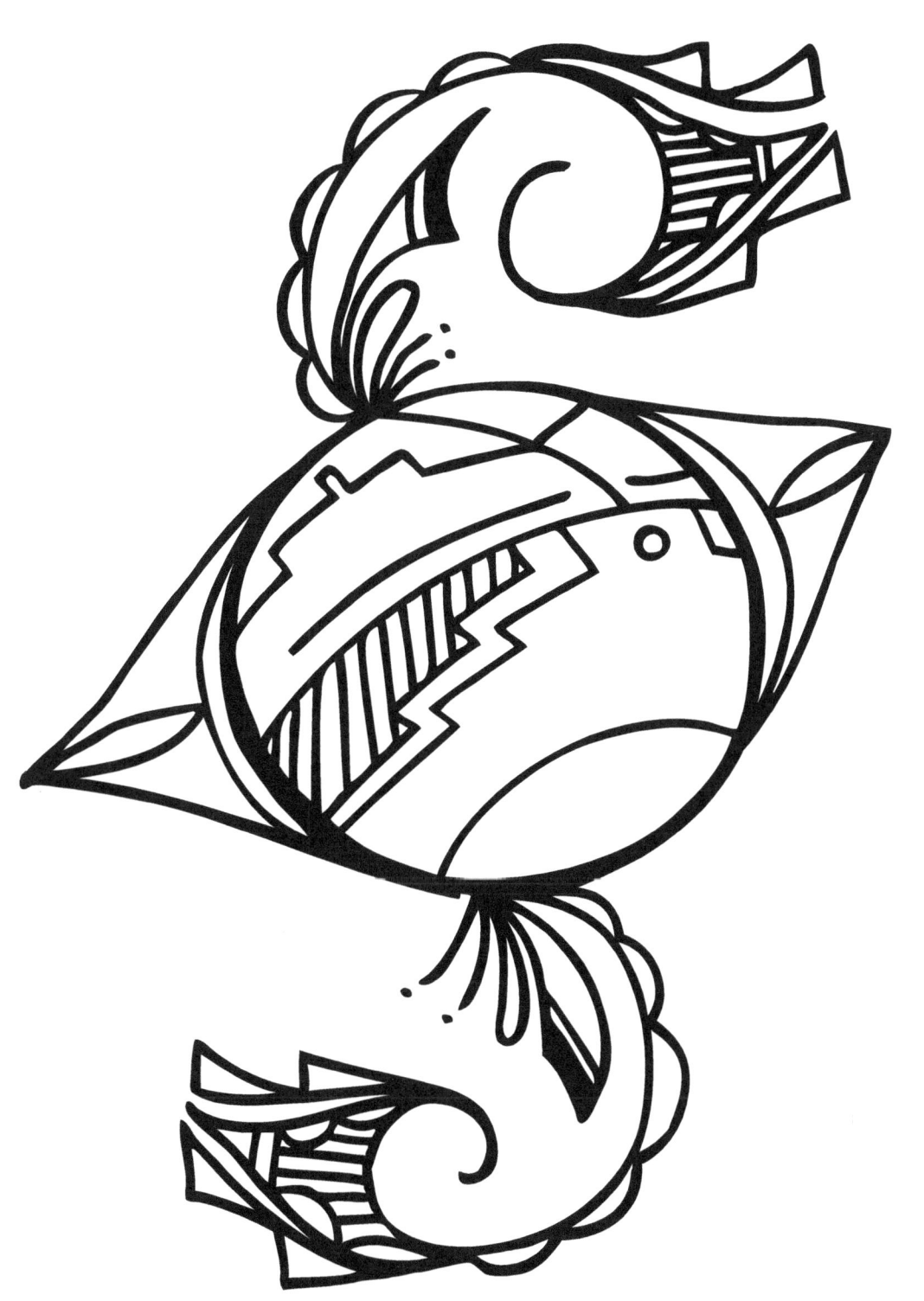

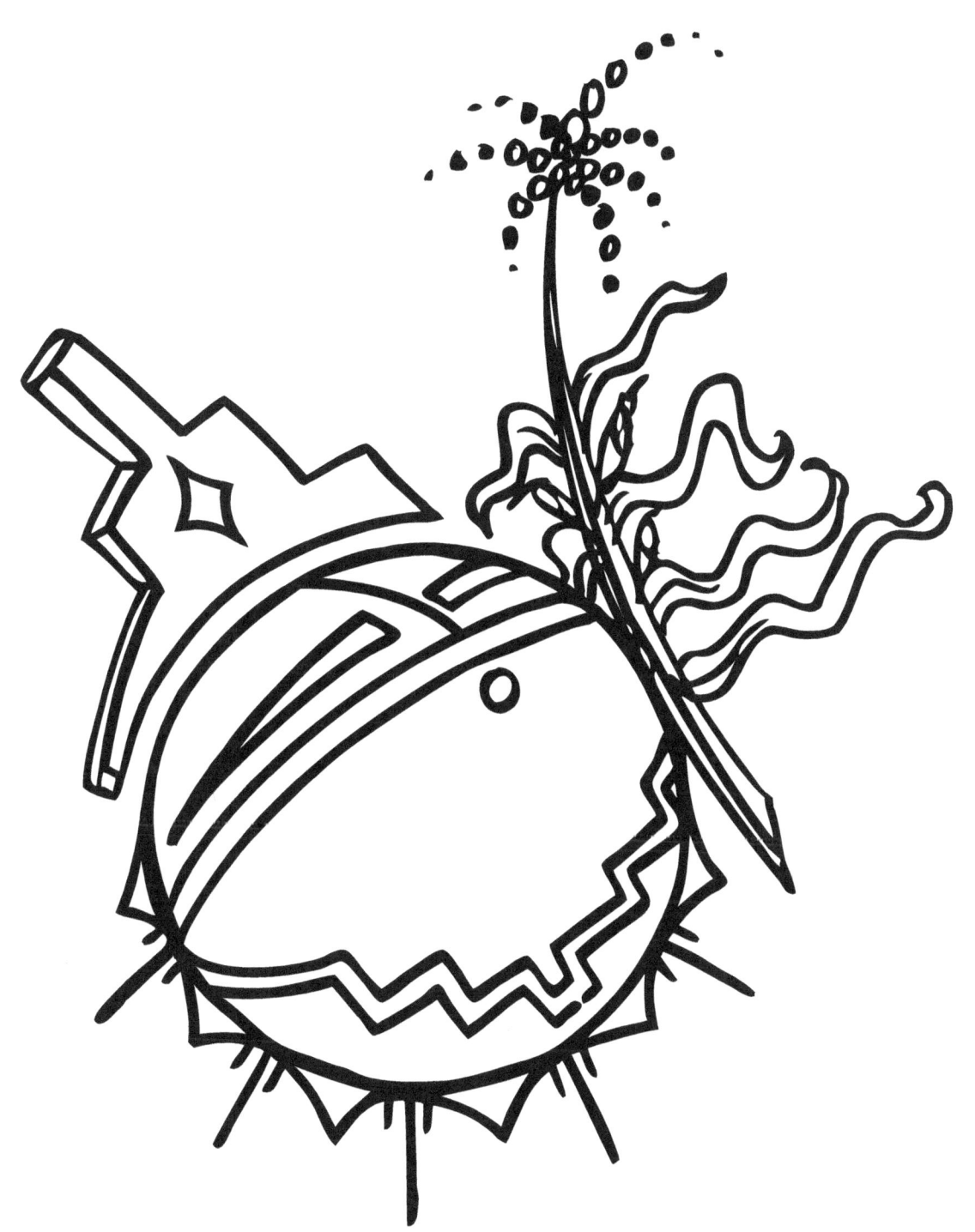

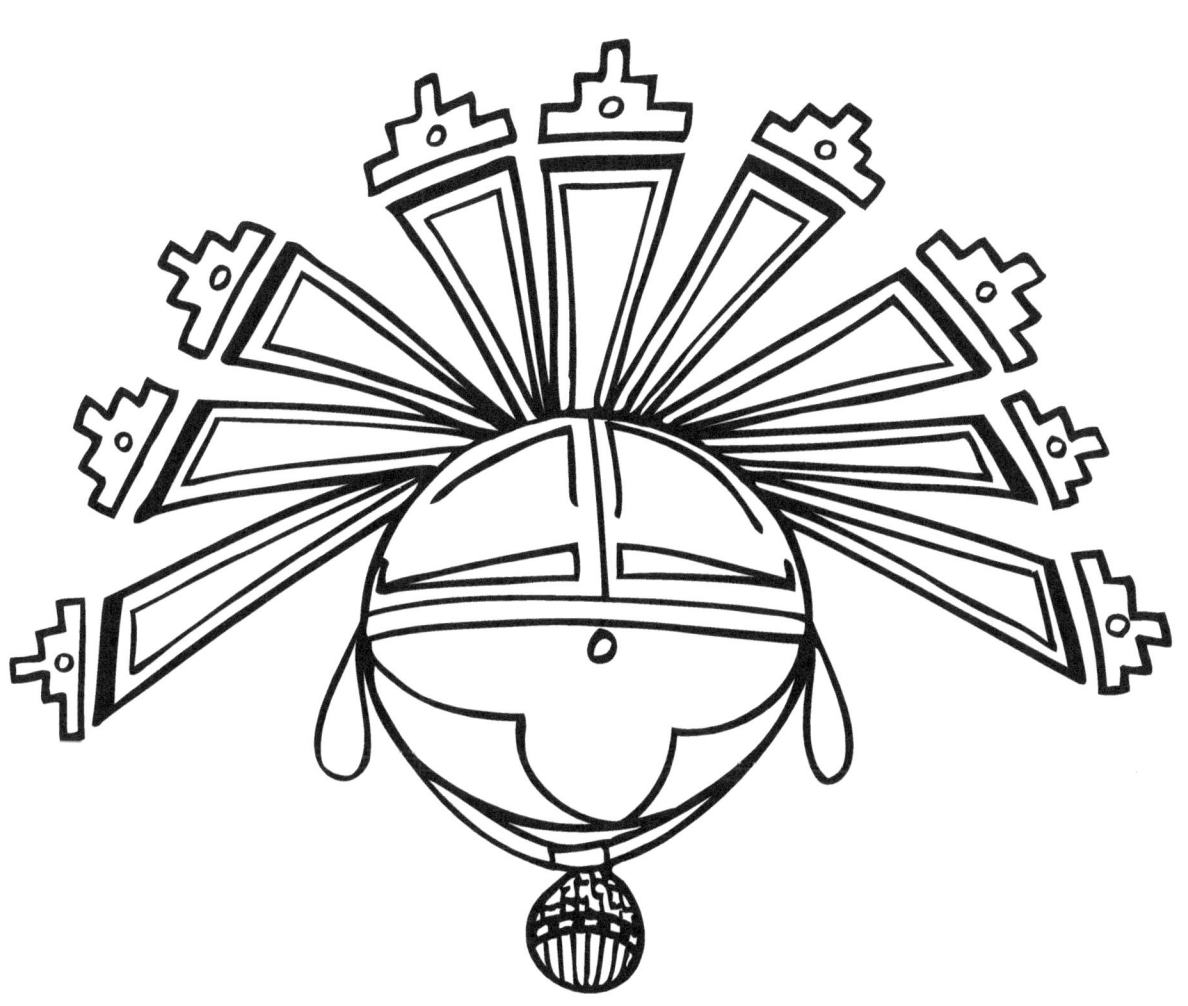

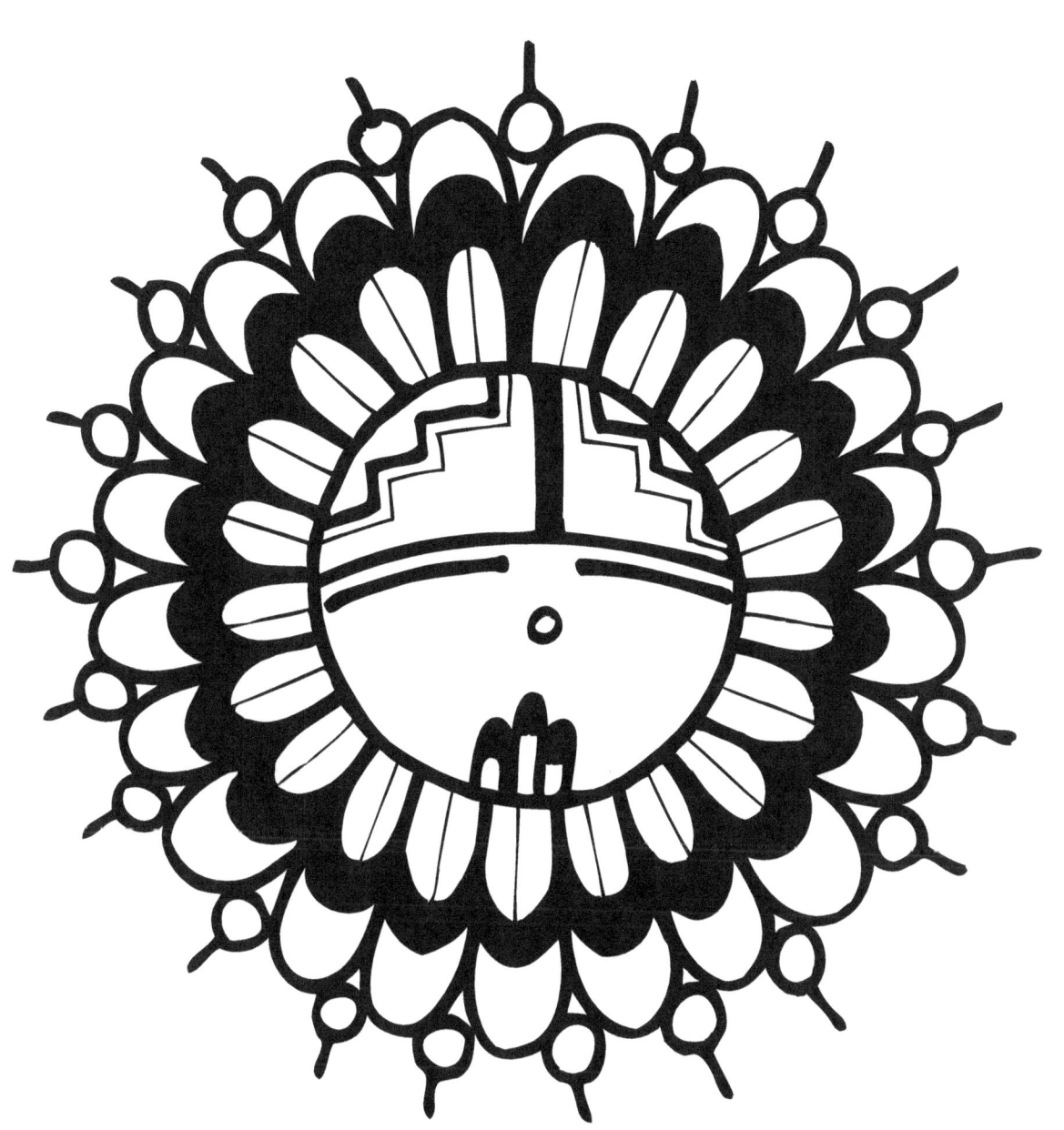

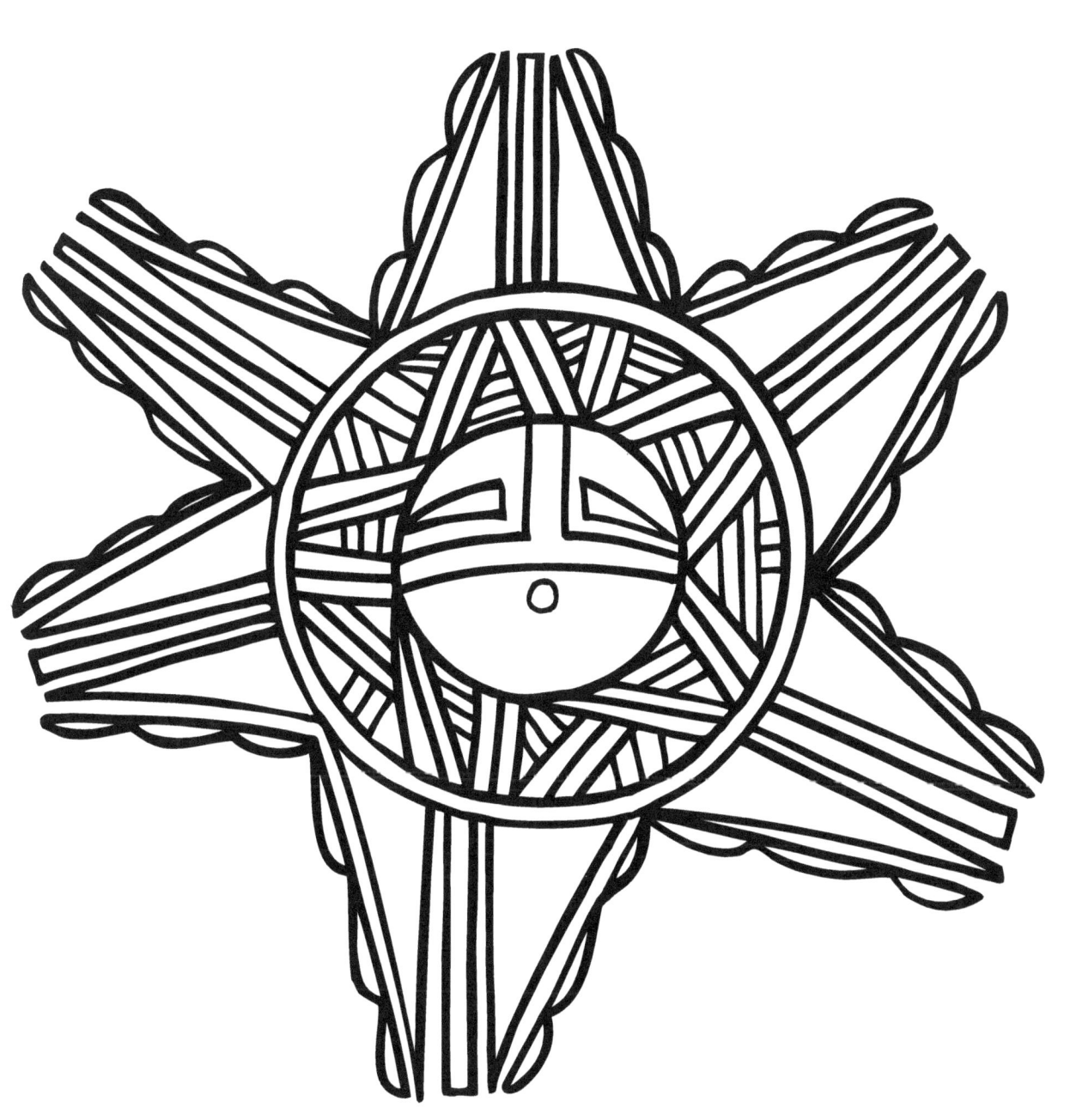

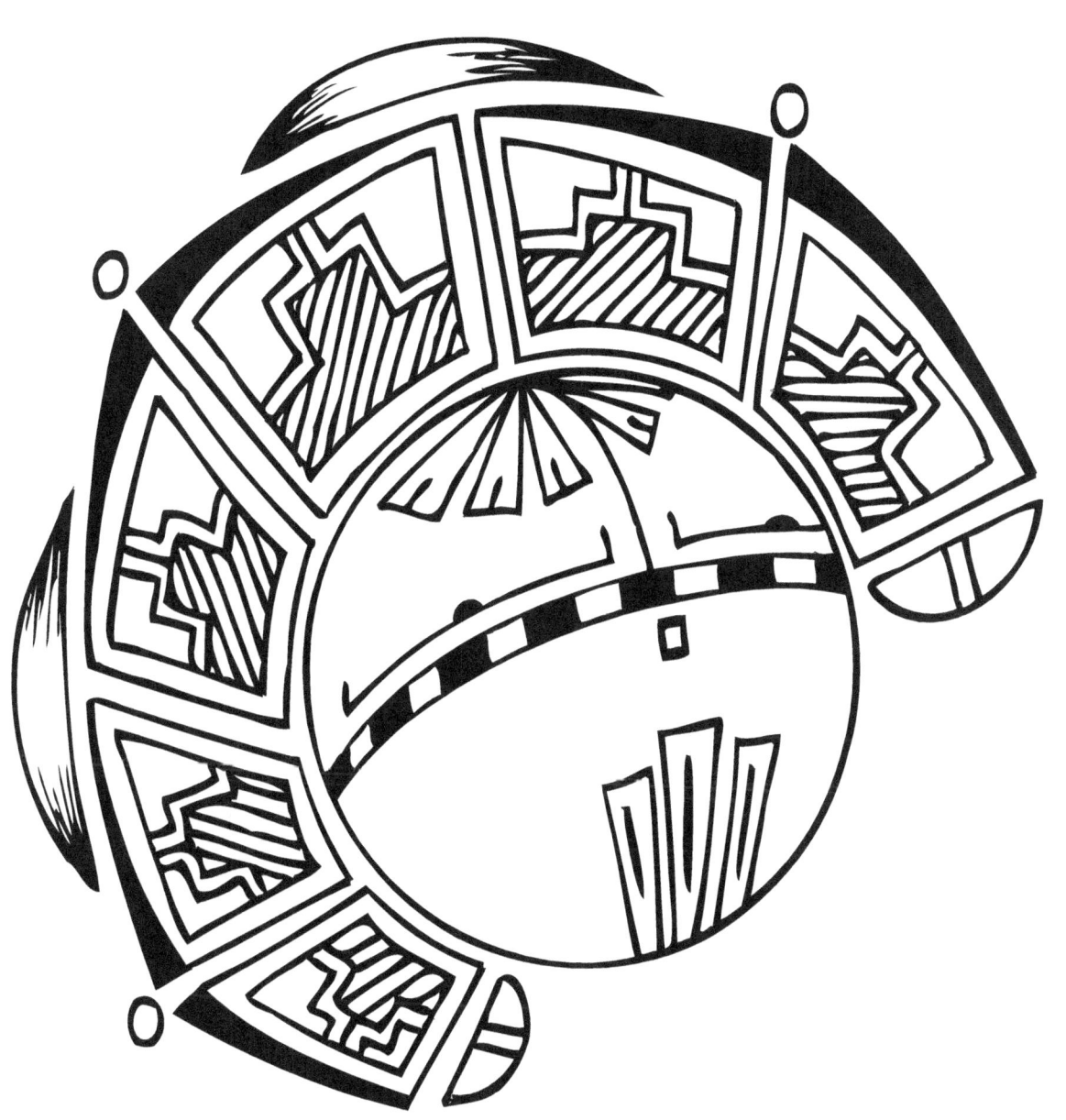

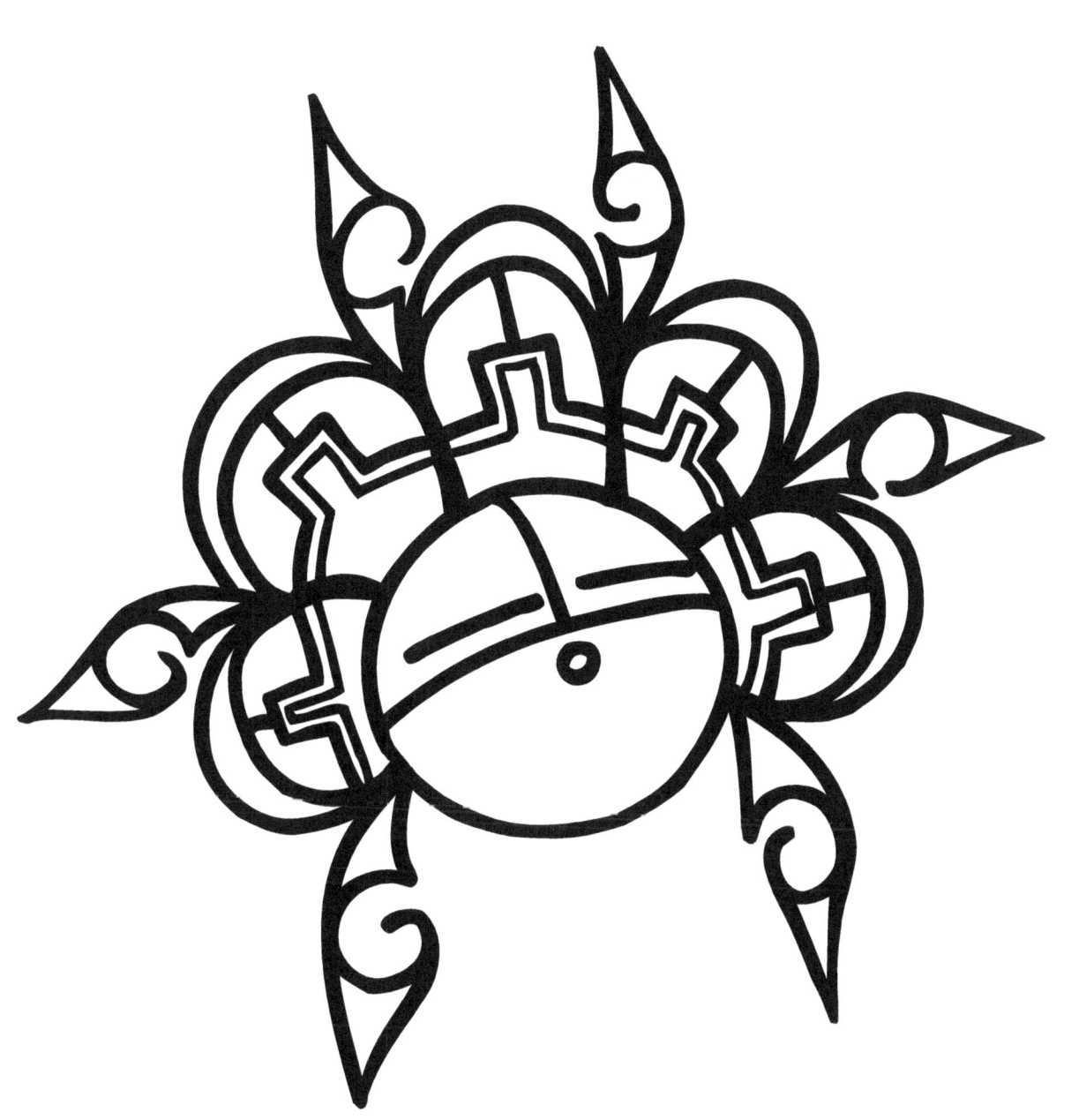

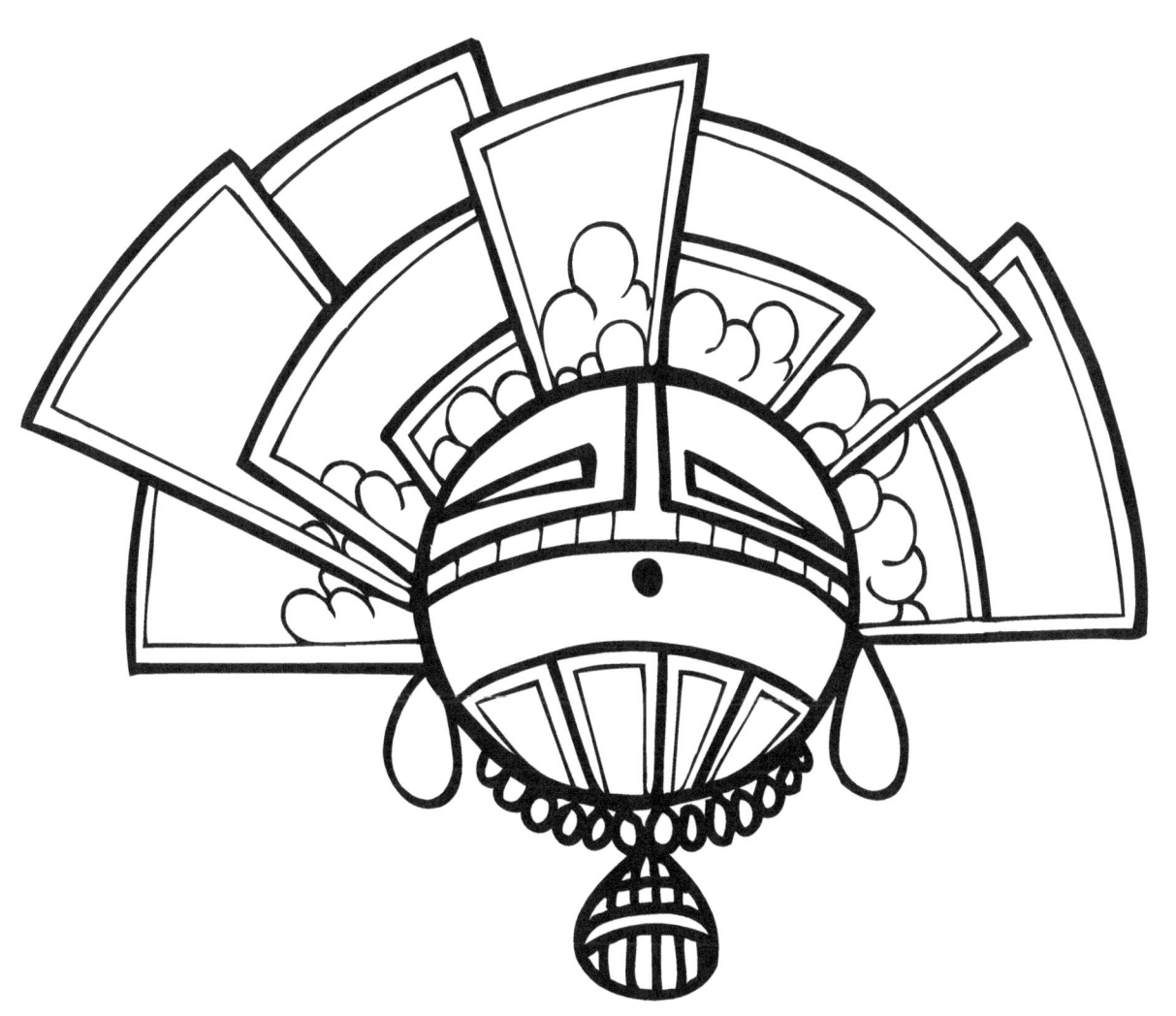

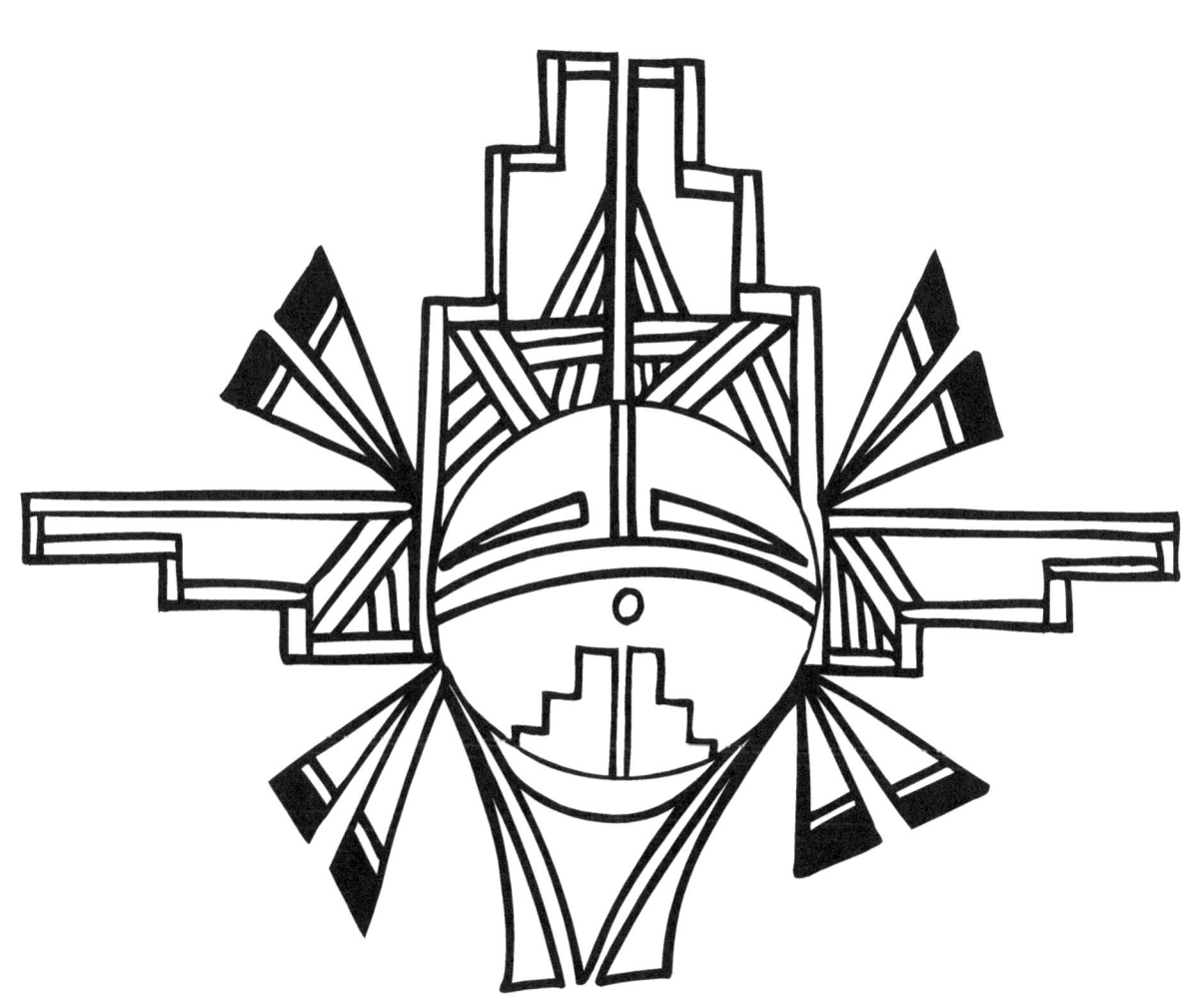

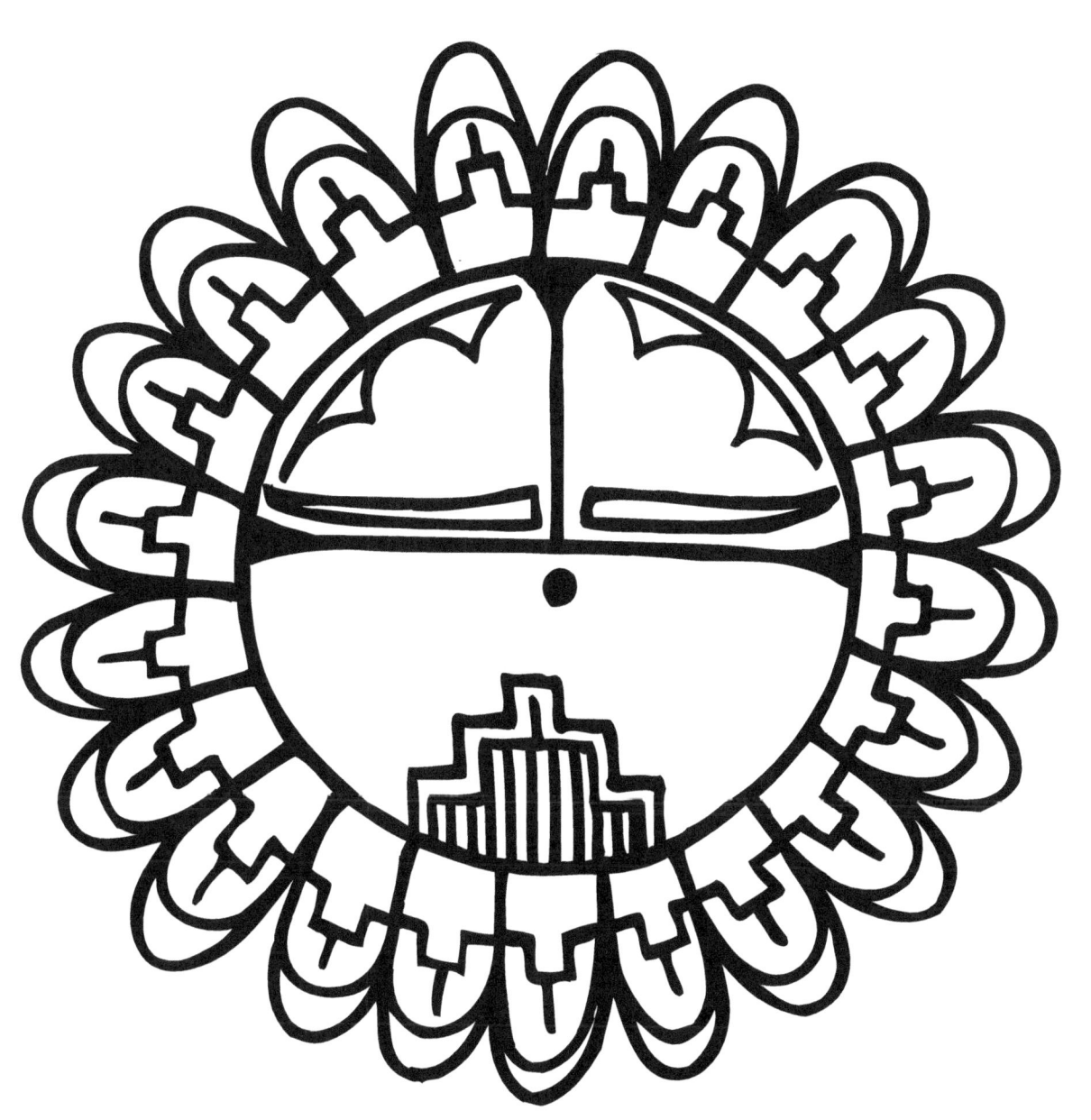

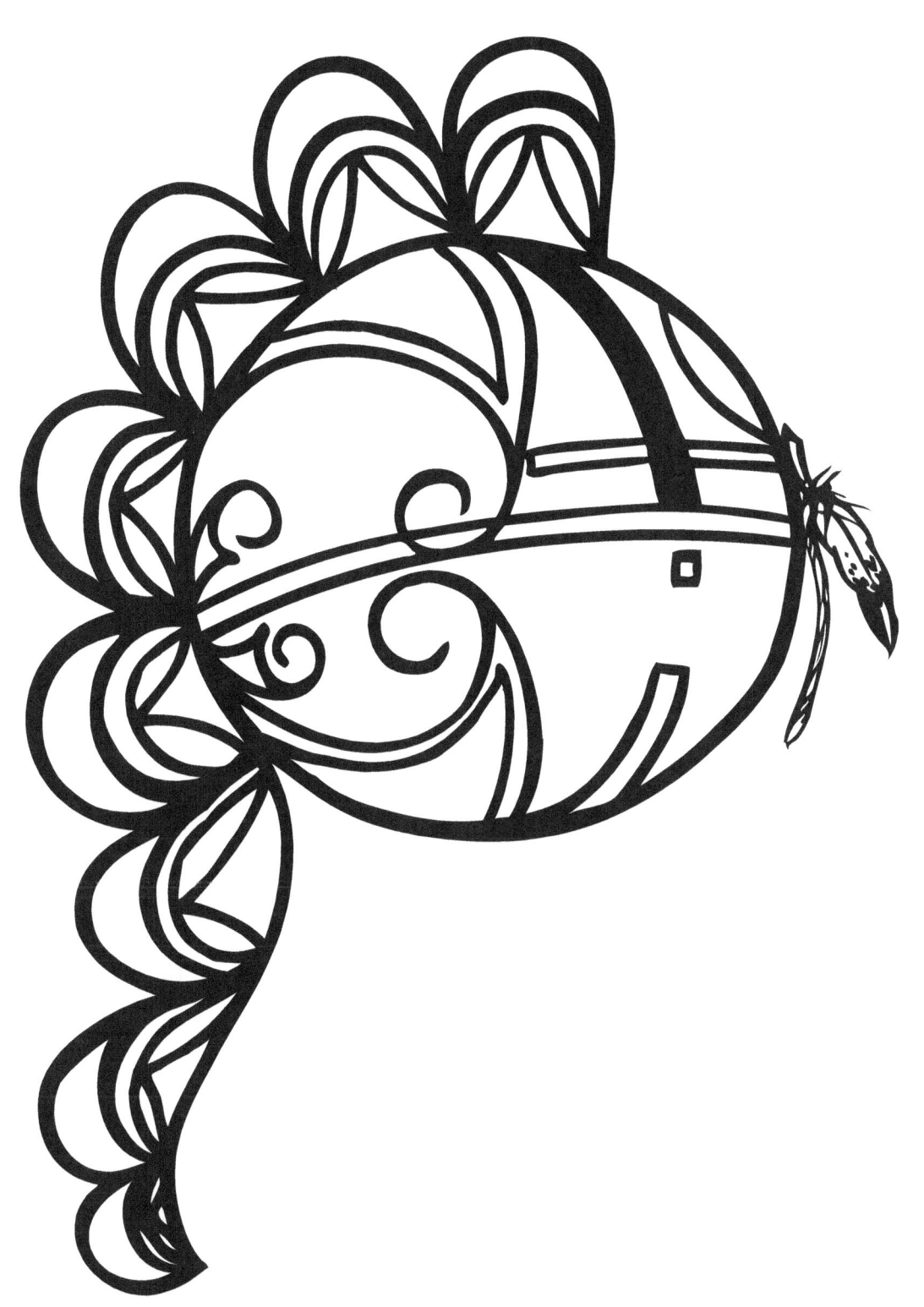

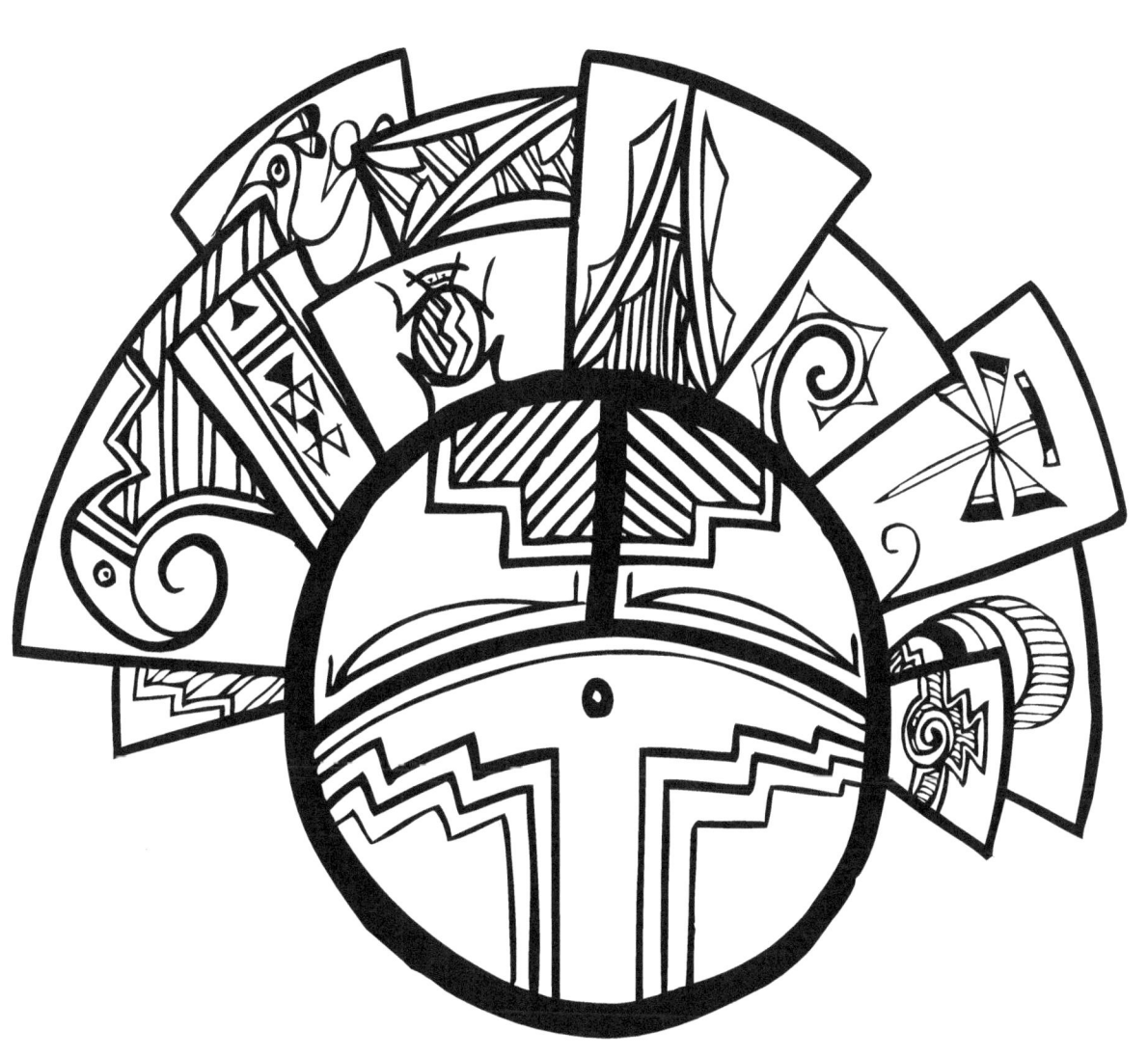

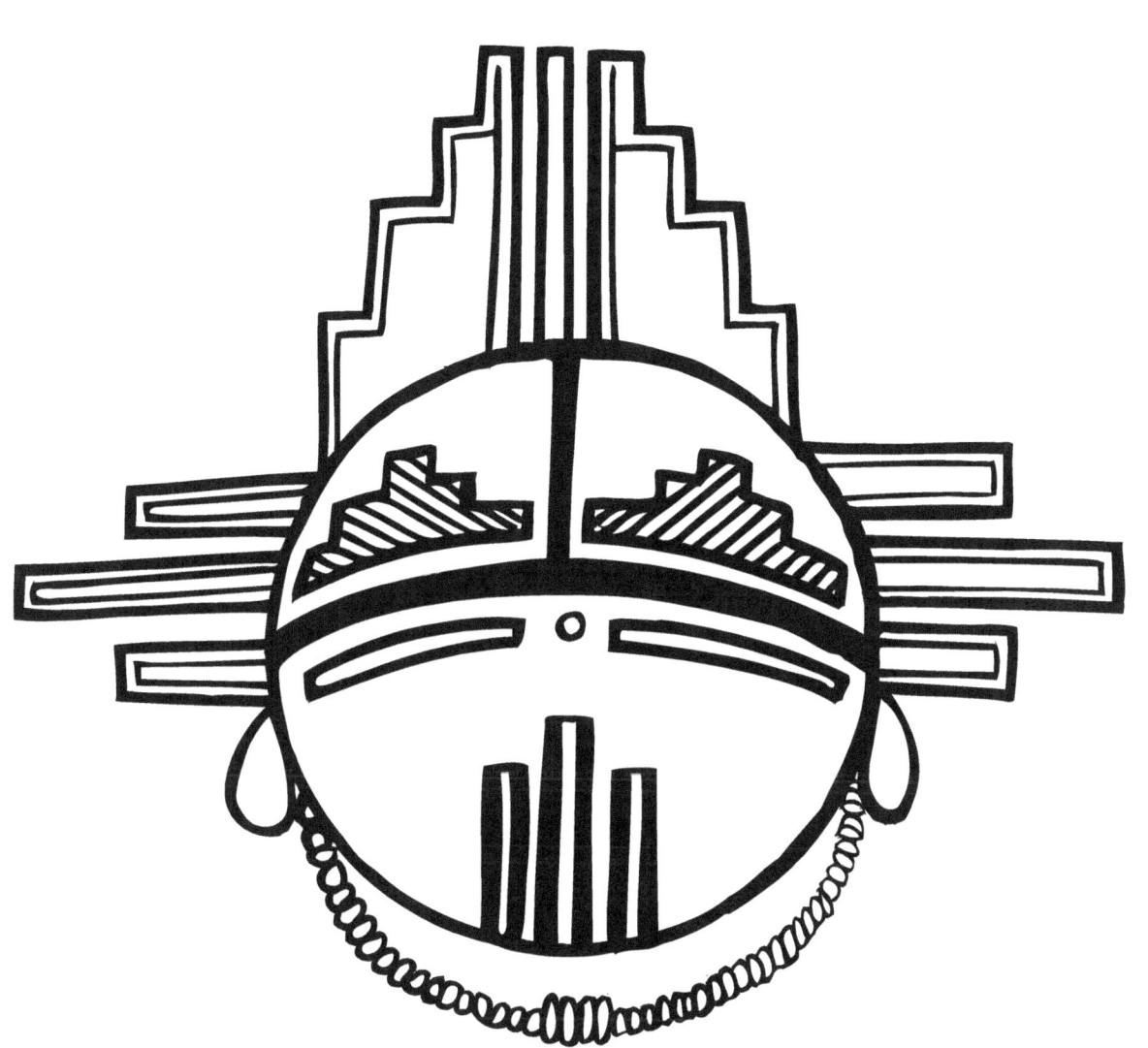

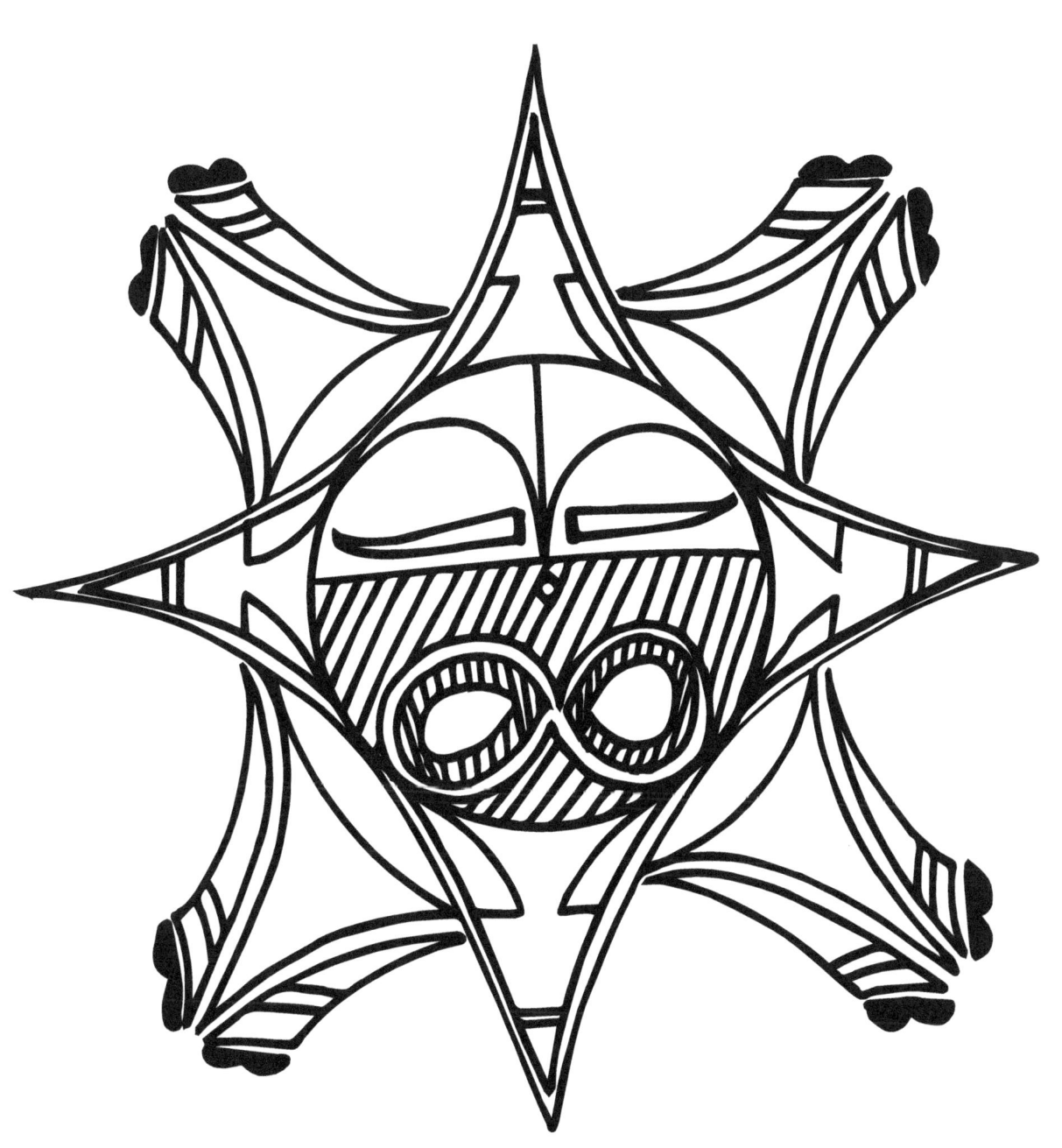

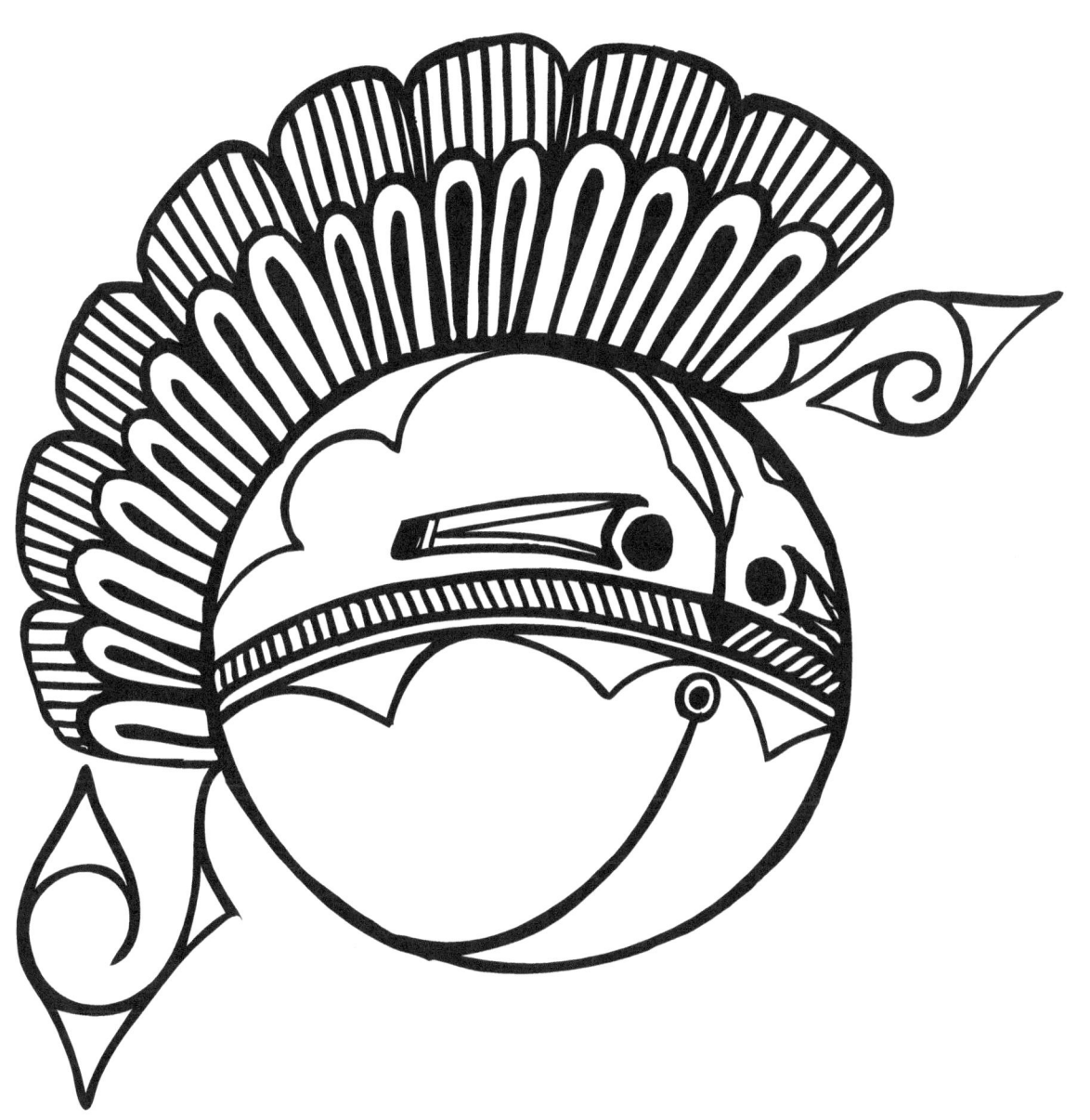

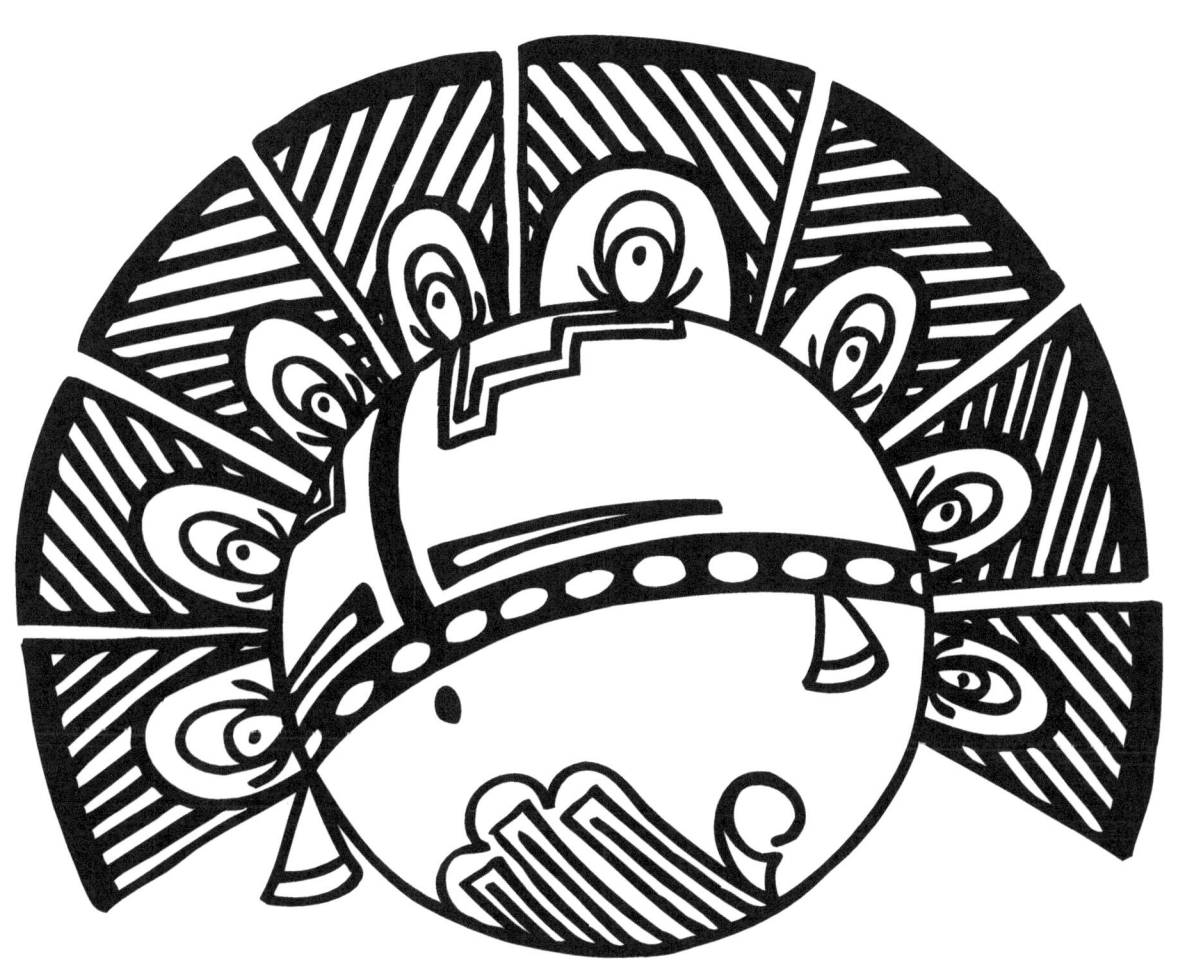

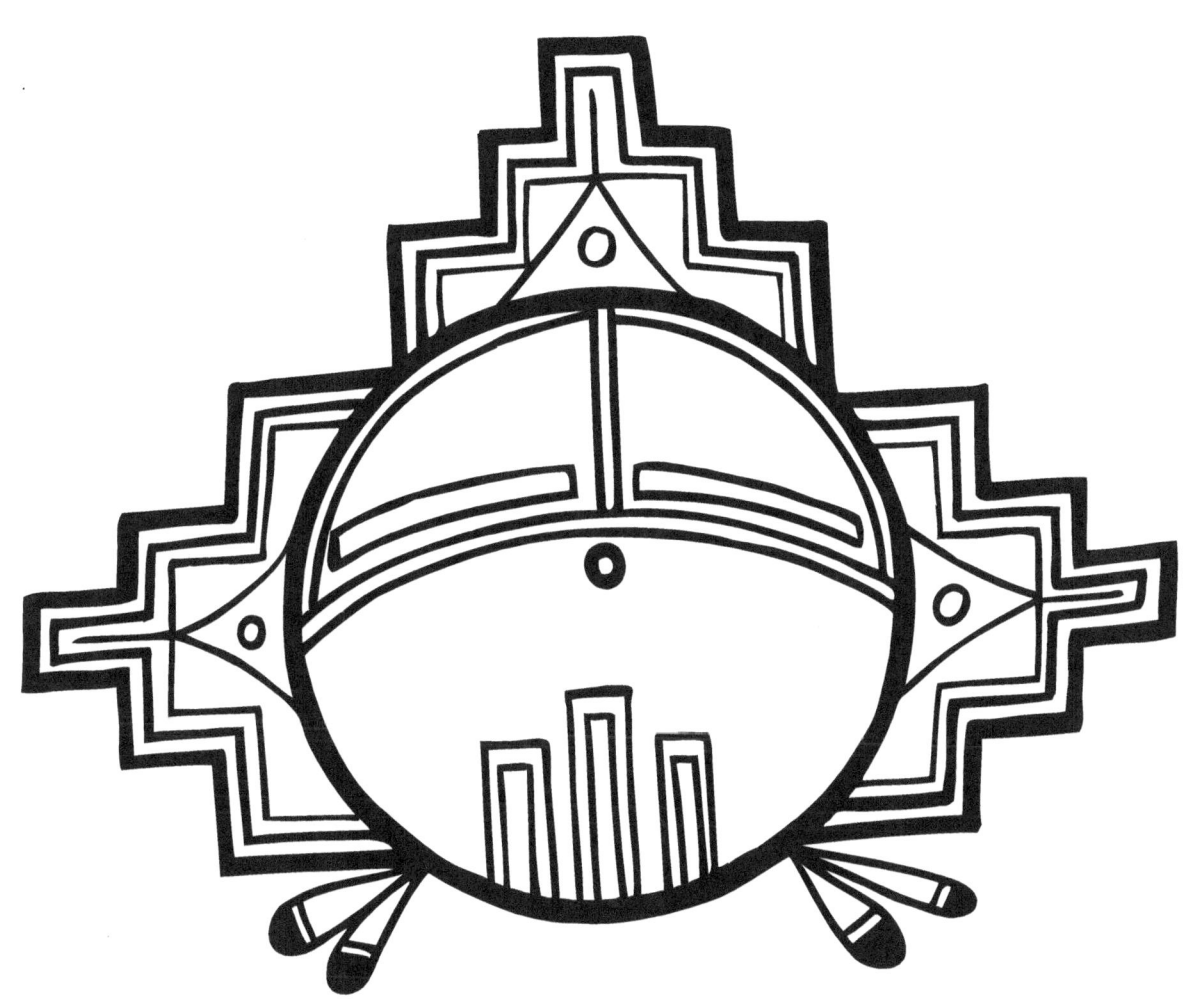

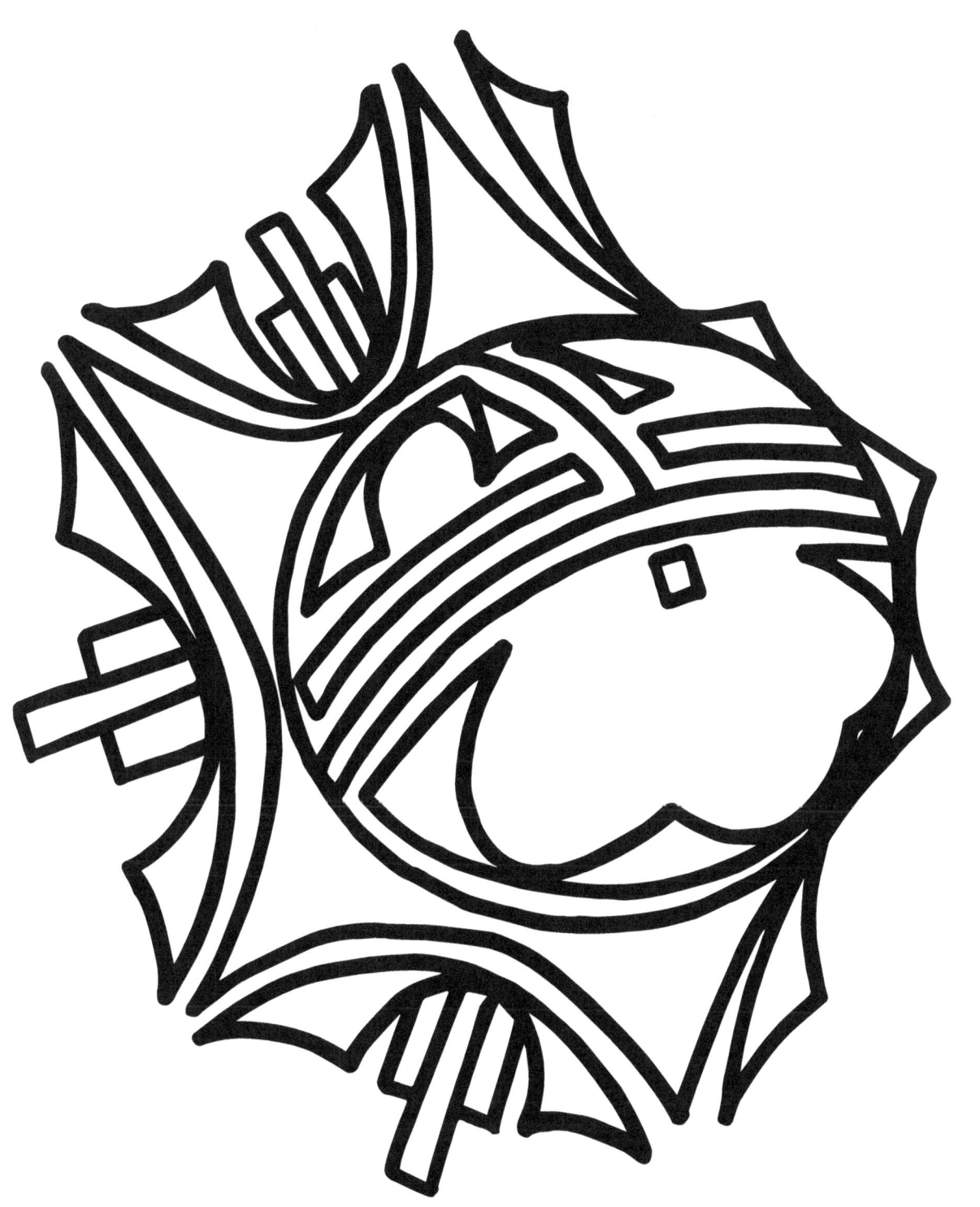

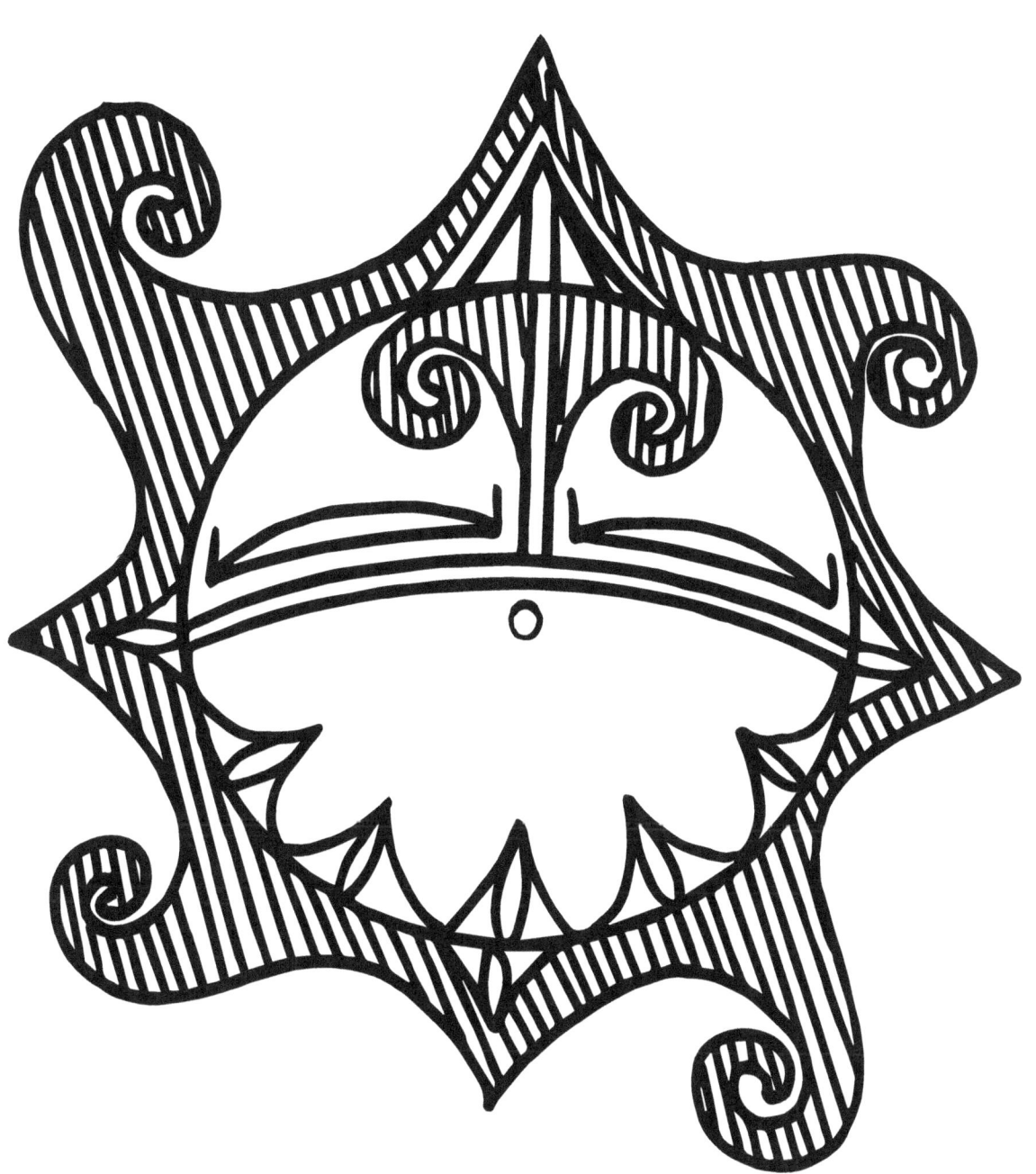

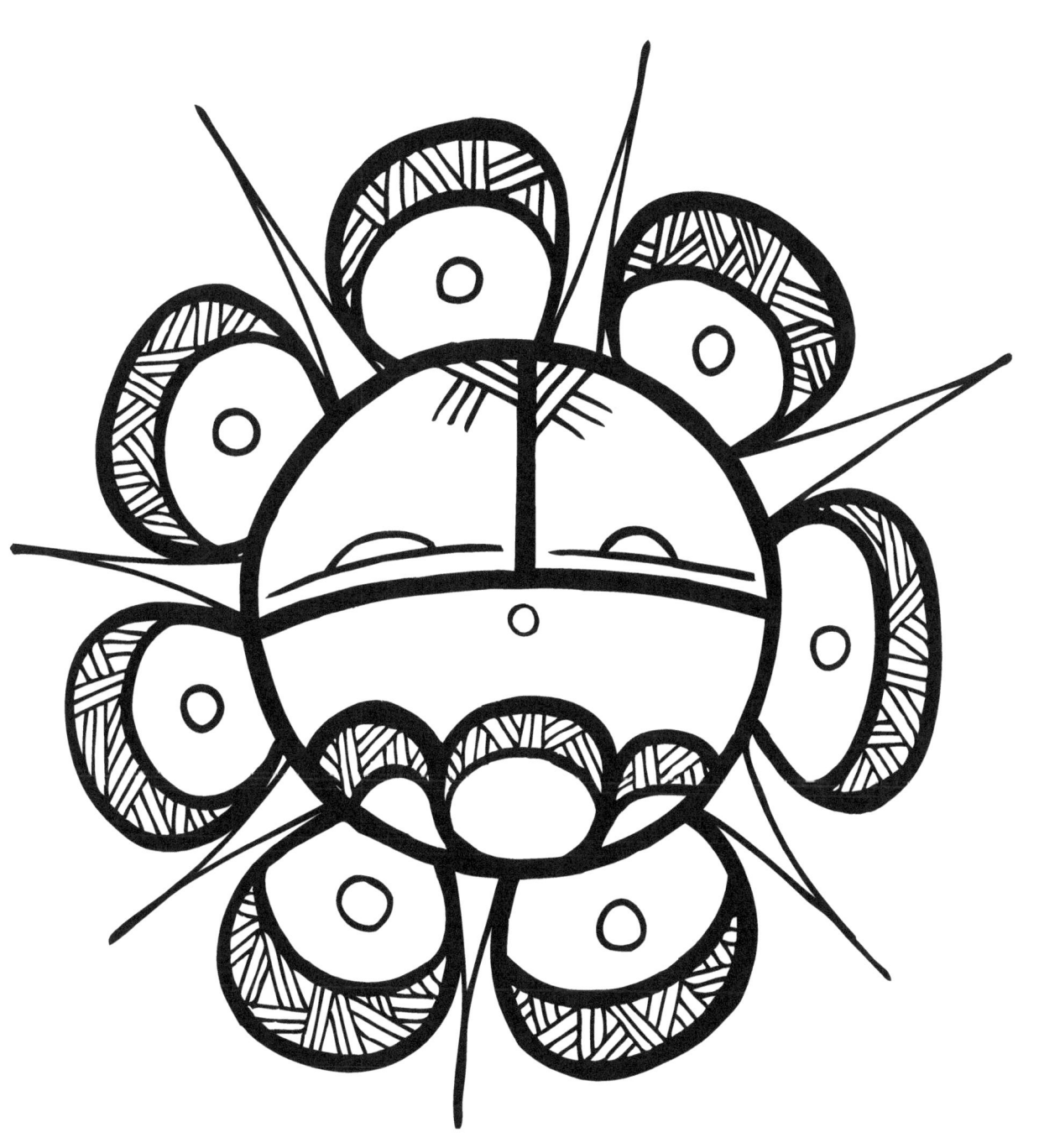

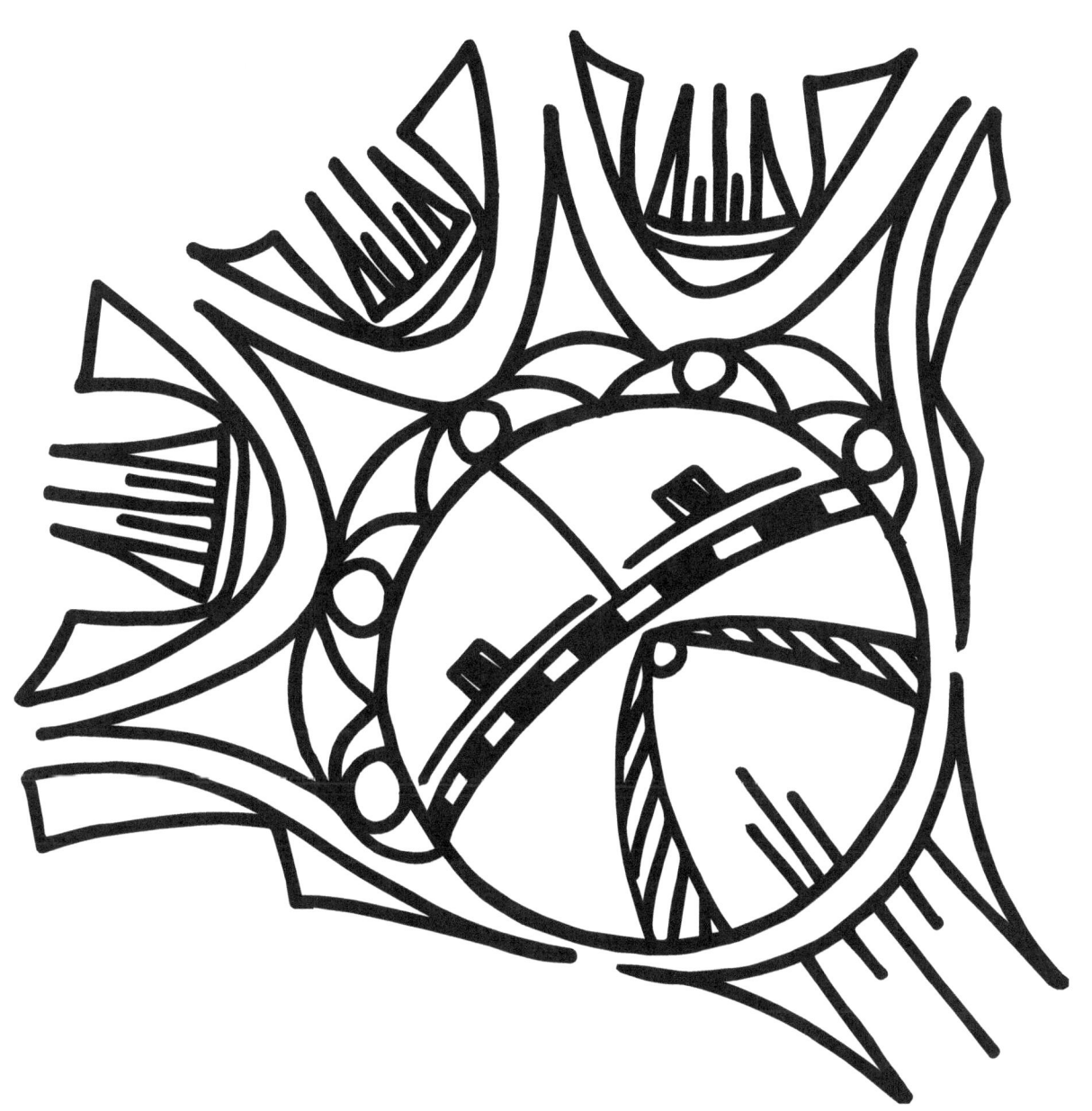

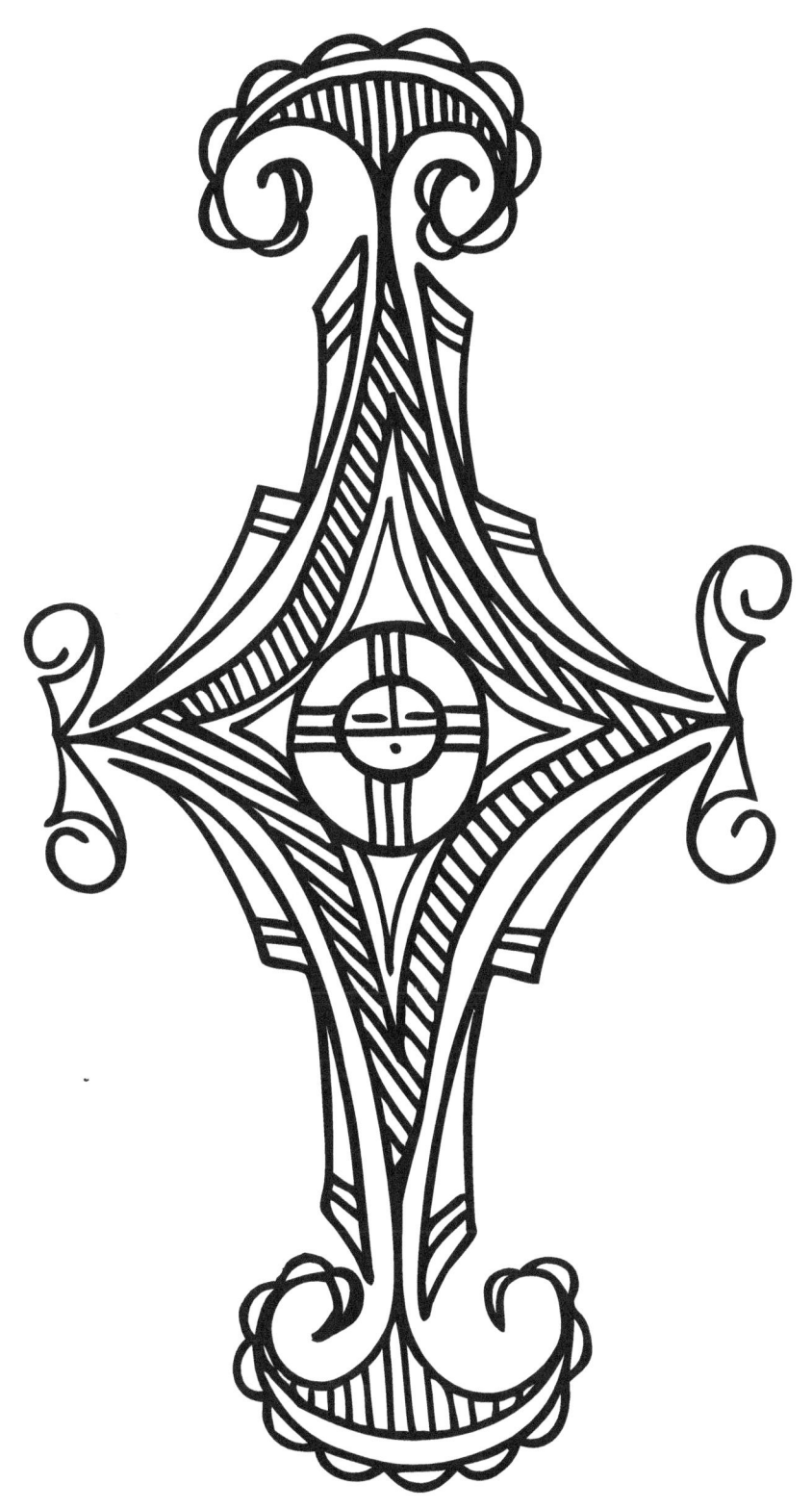

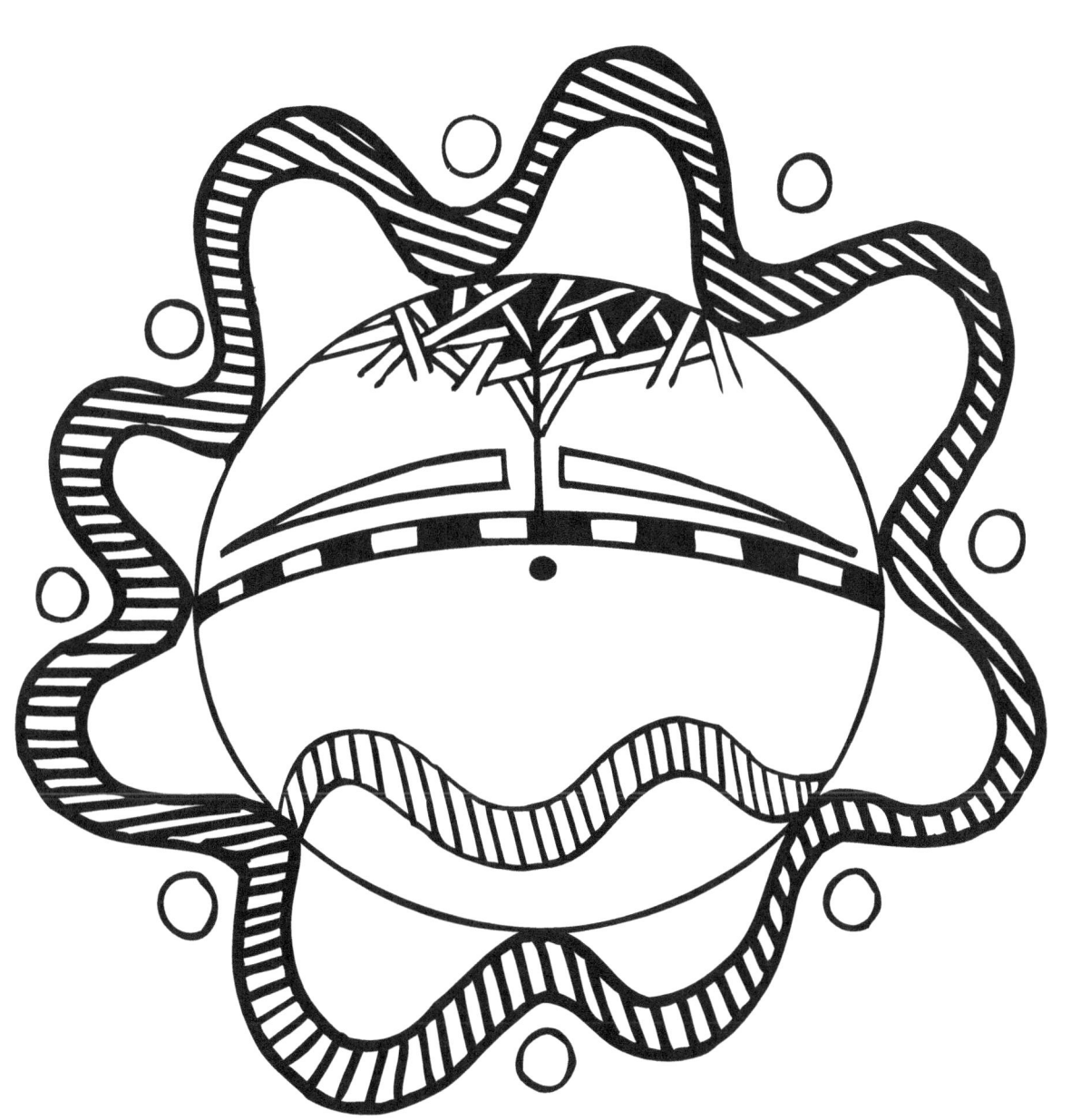

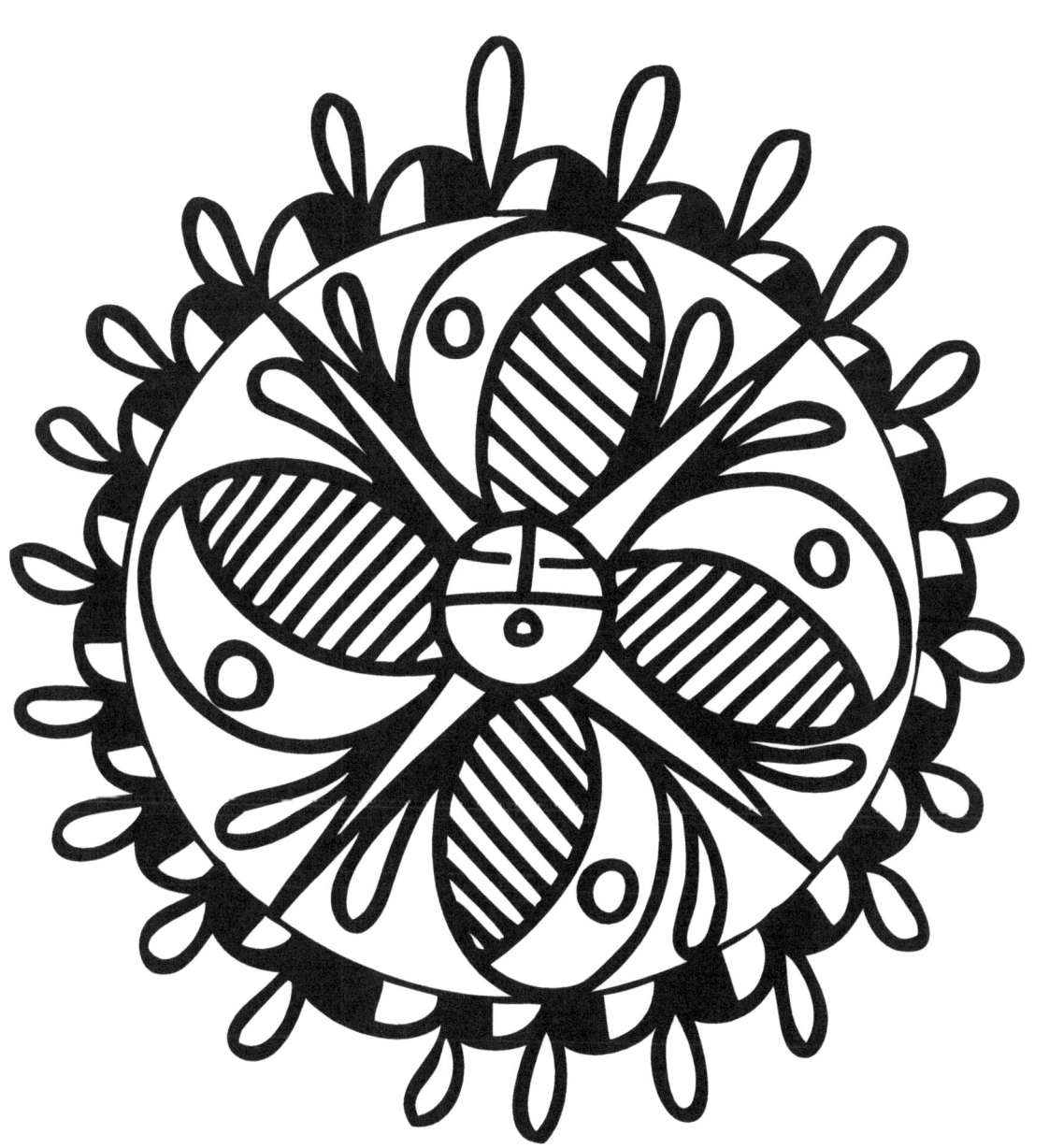

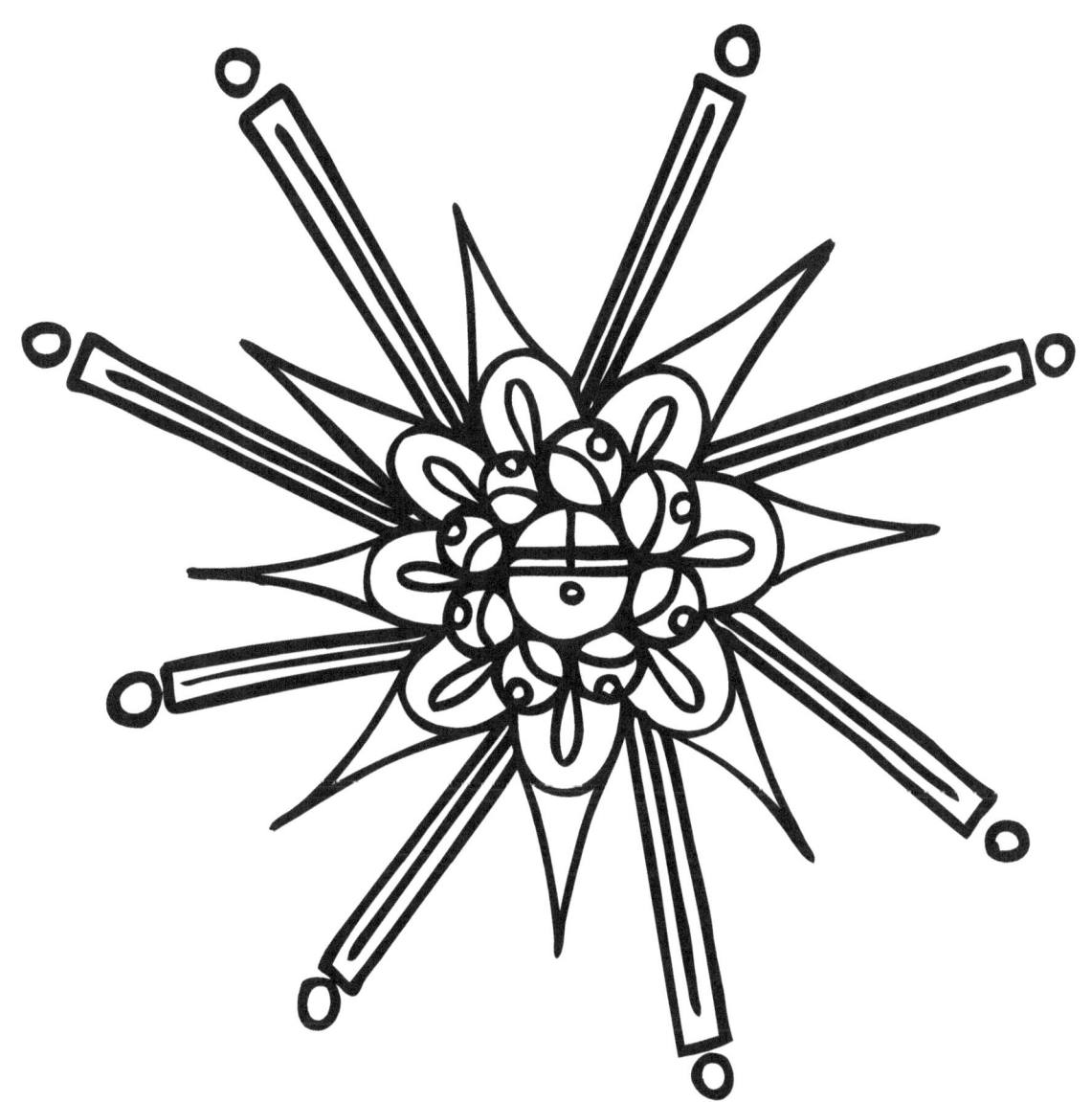

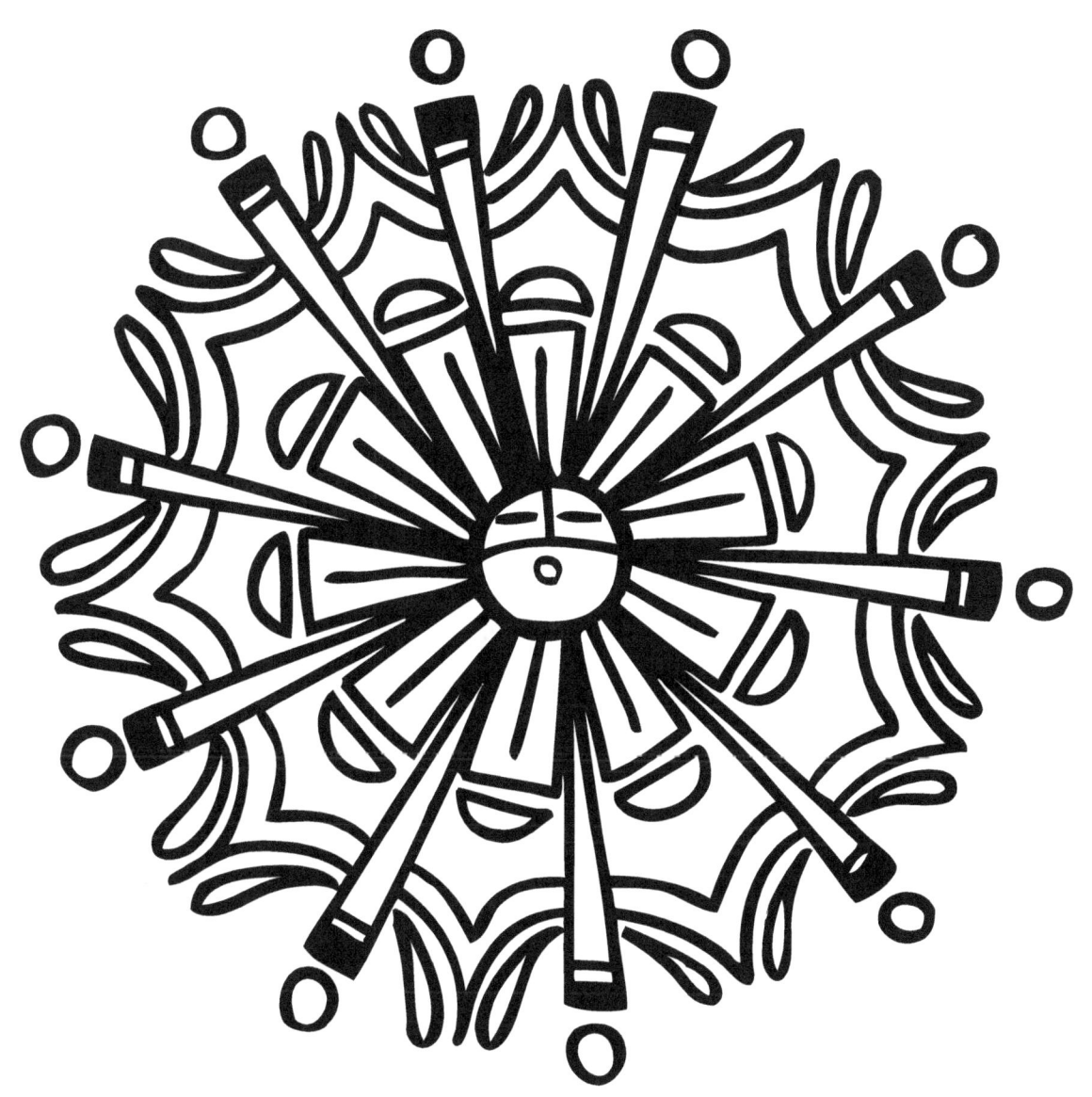

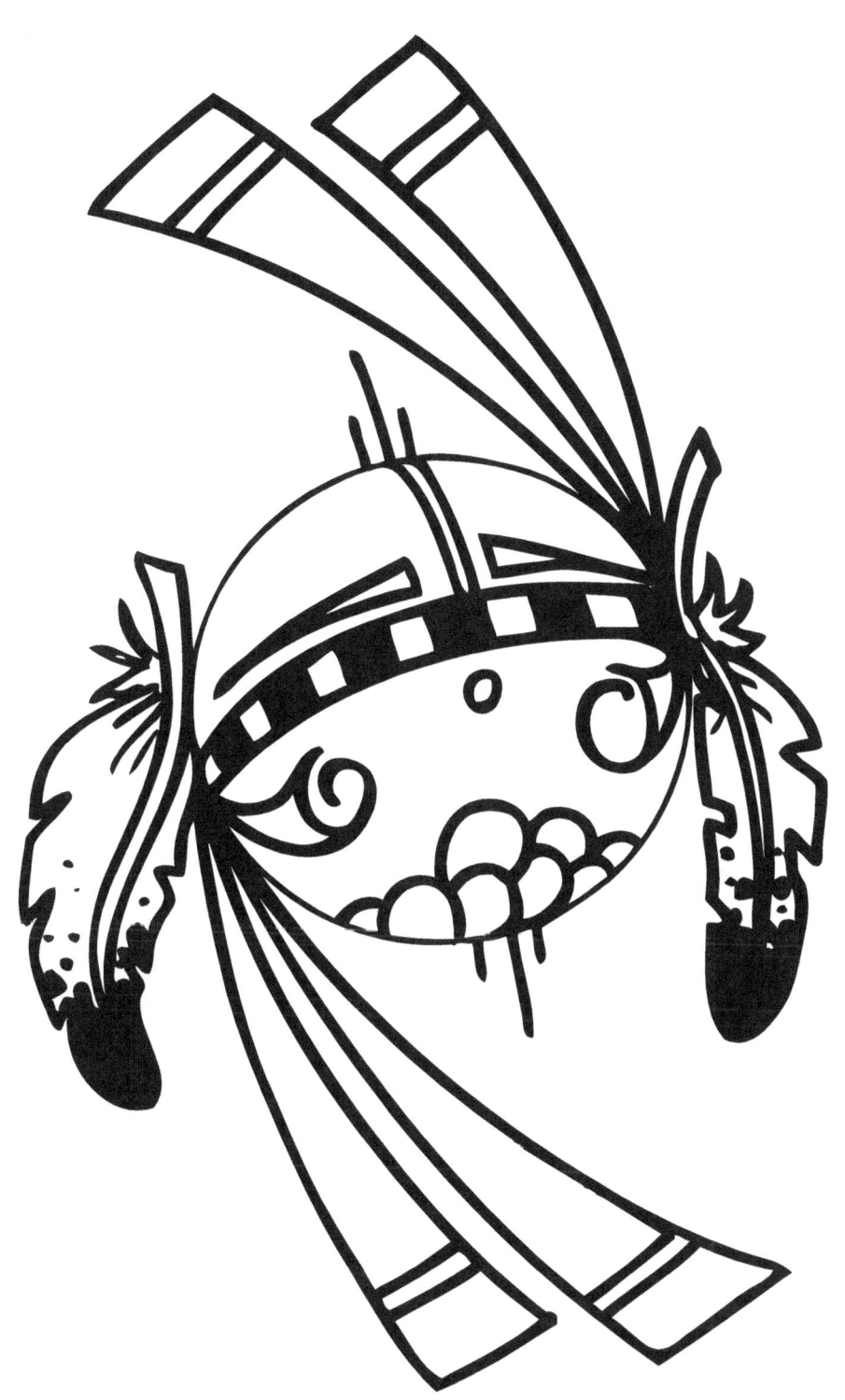

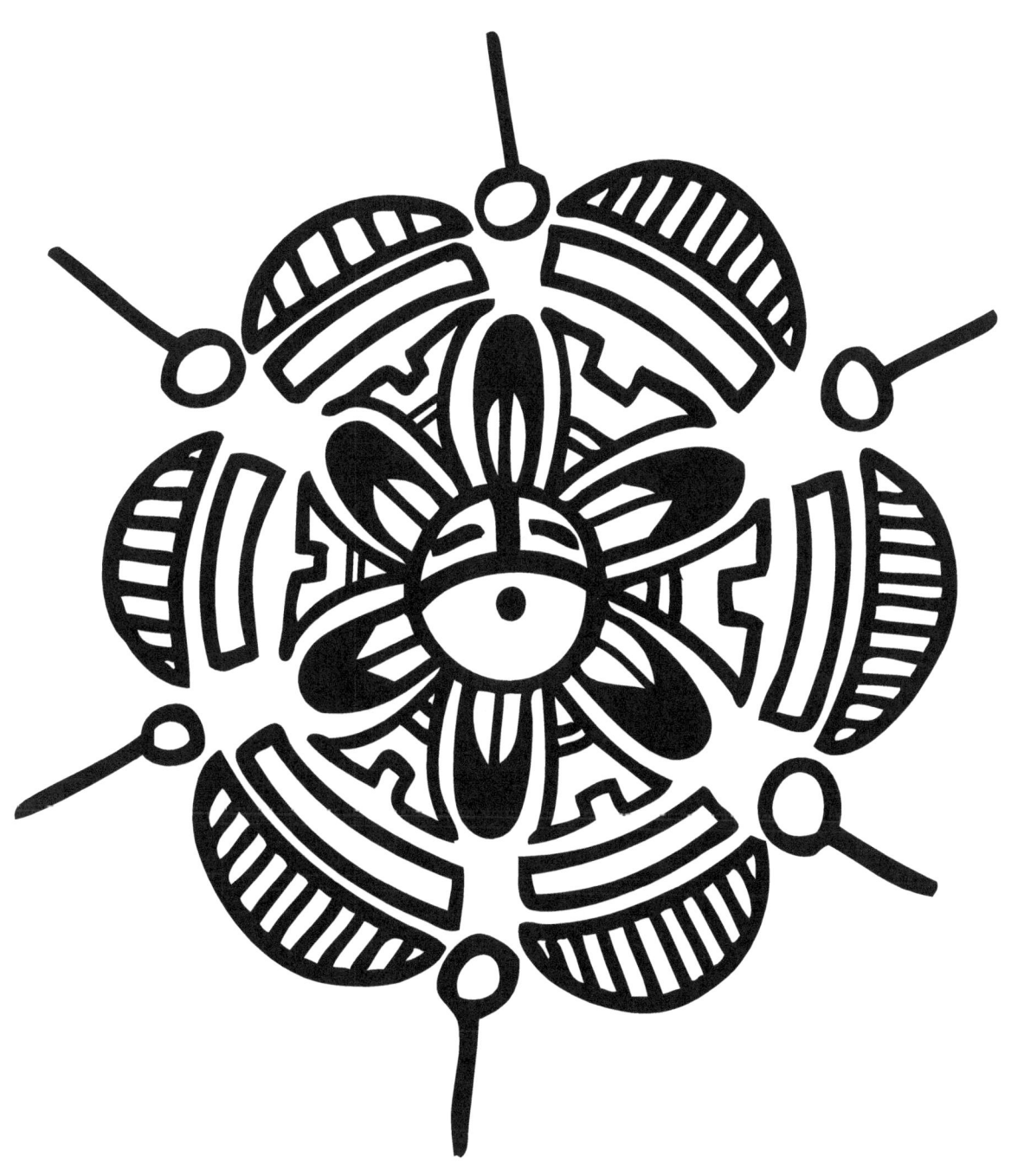

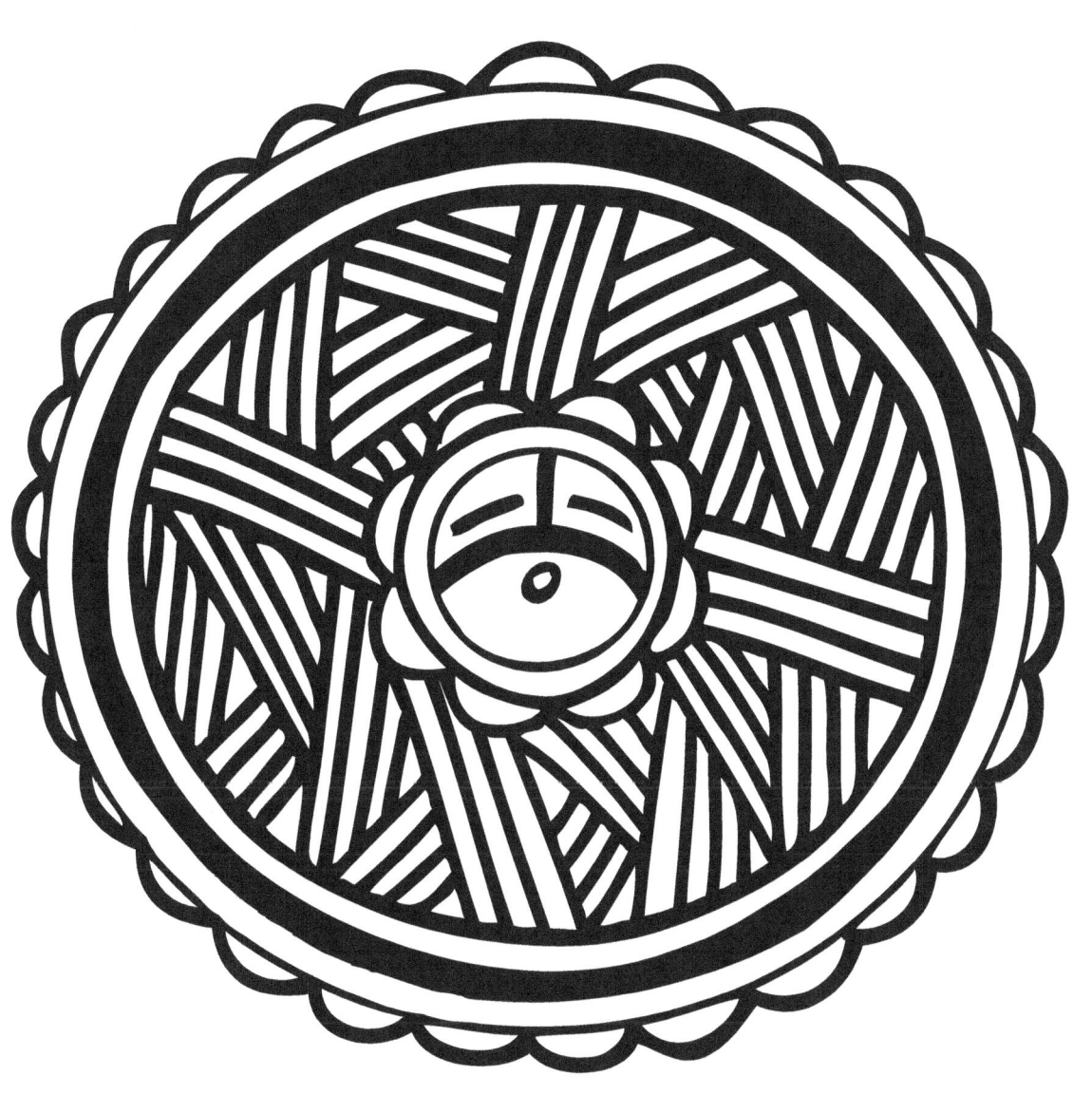

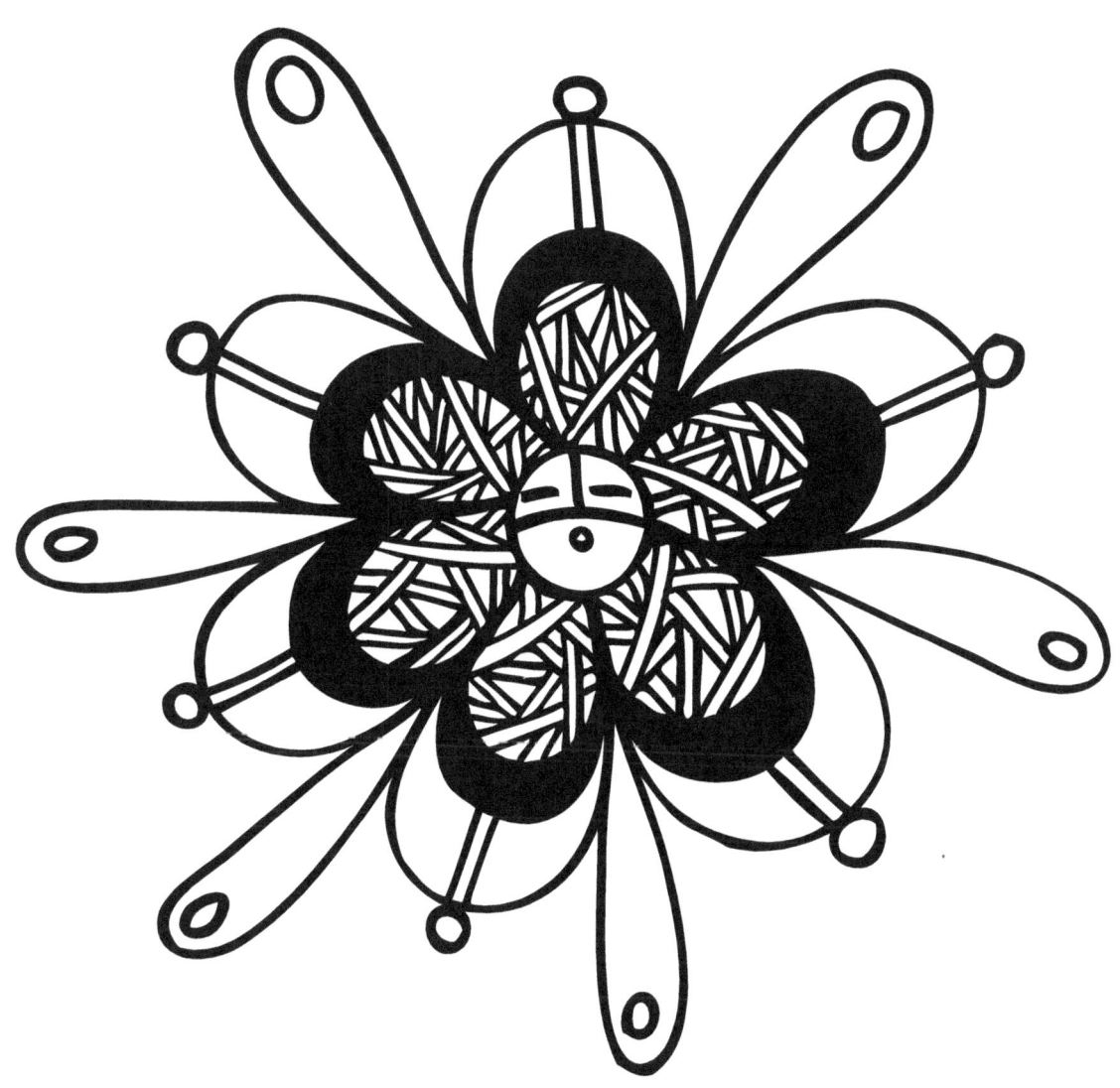

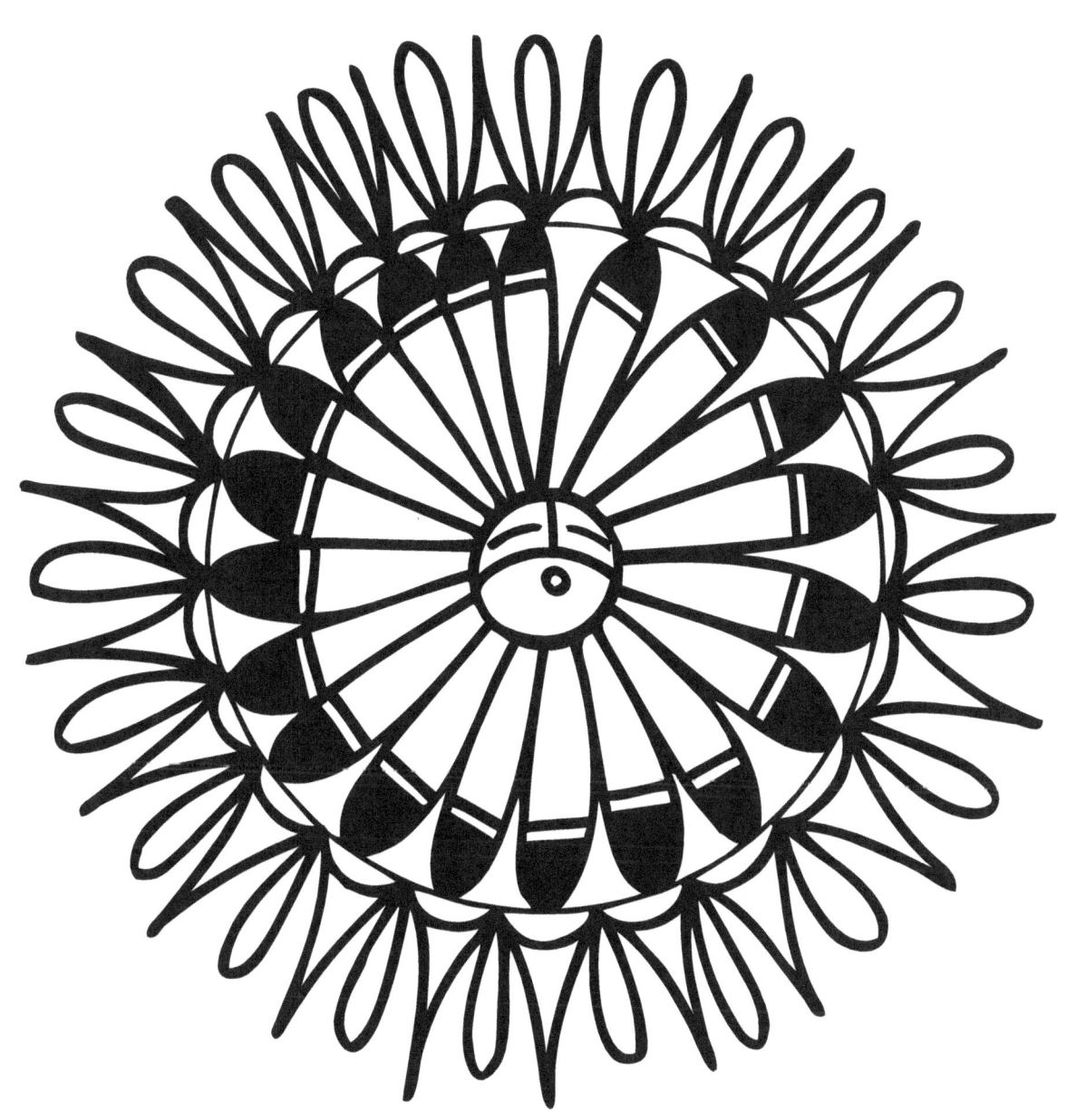

NOW YOUR TURN. DESIGN YOUR OWN SUNFACE.

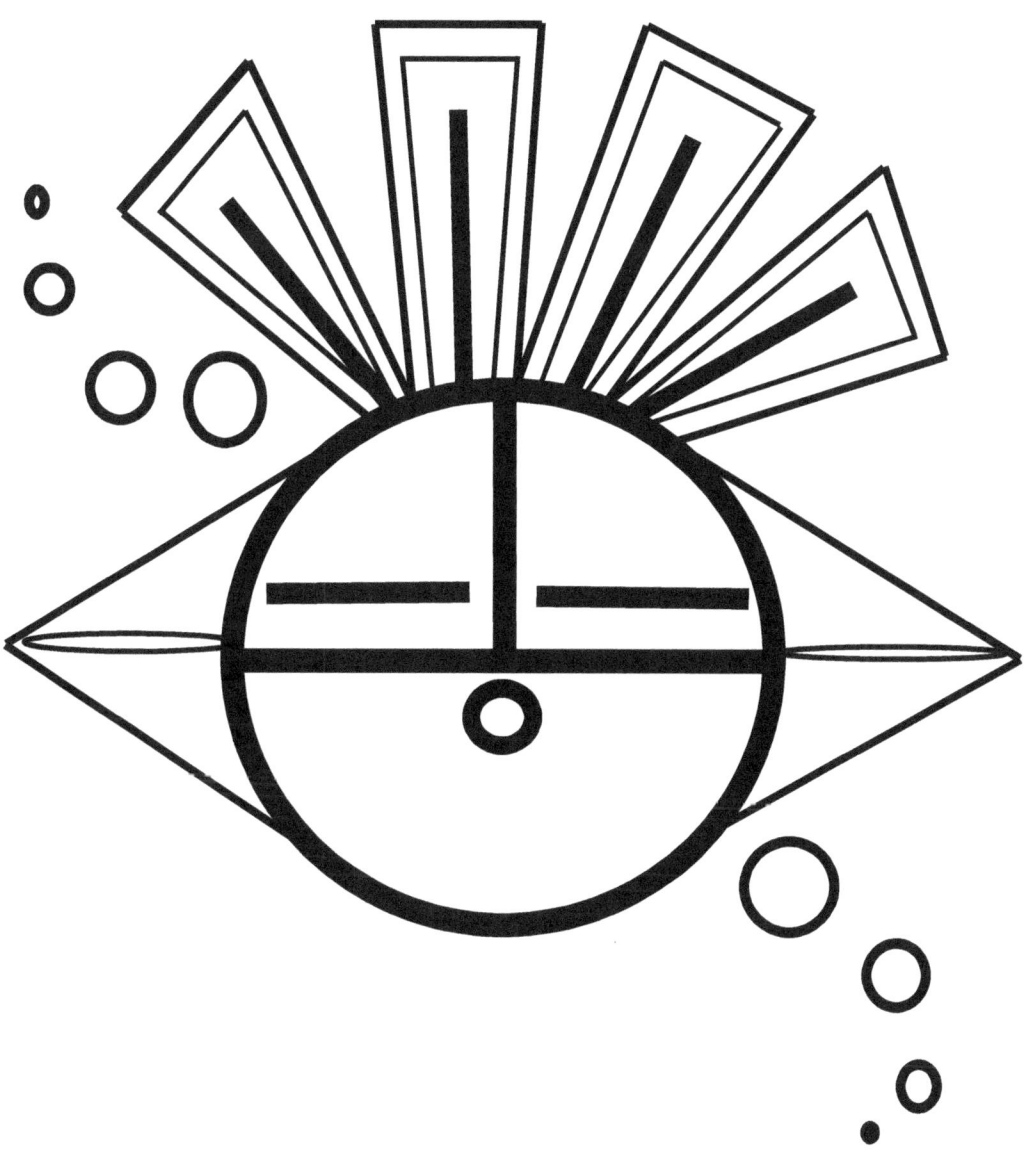

SHARE YOUR CREATIONS WITH EVERYONE!!!

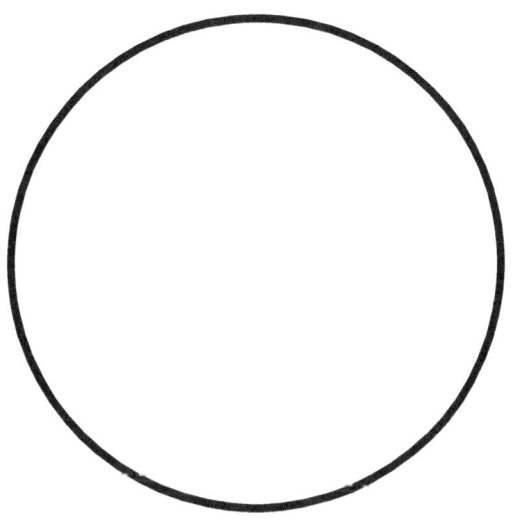

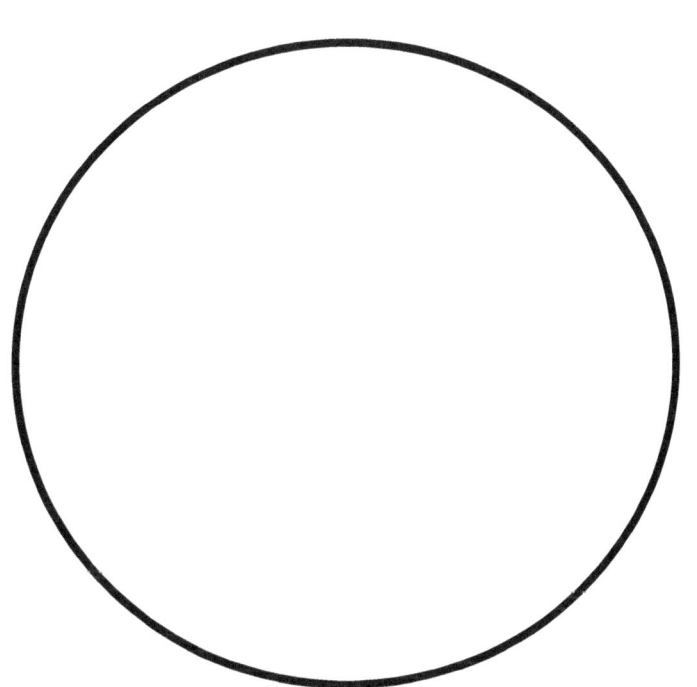

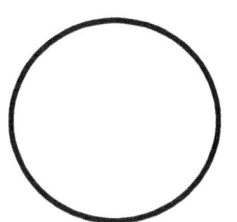

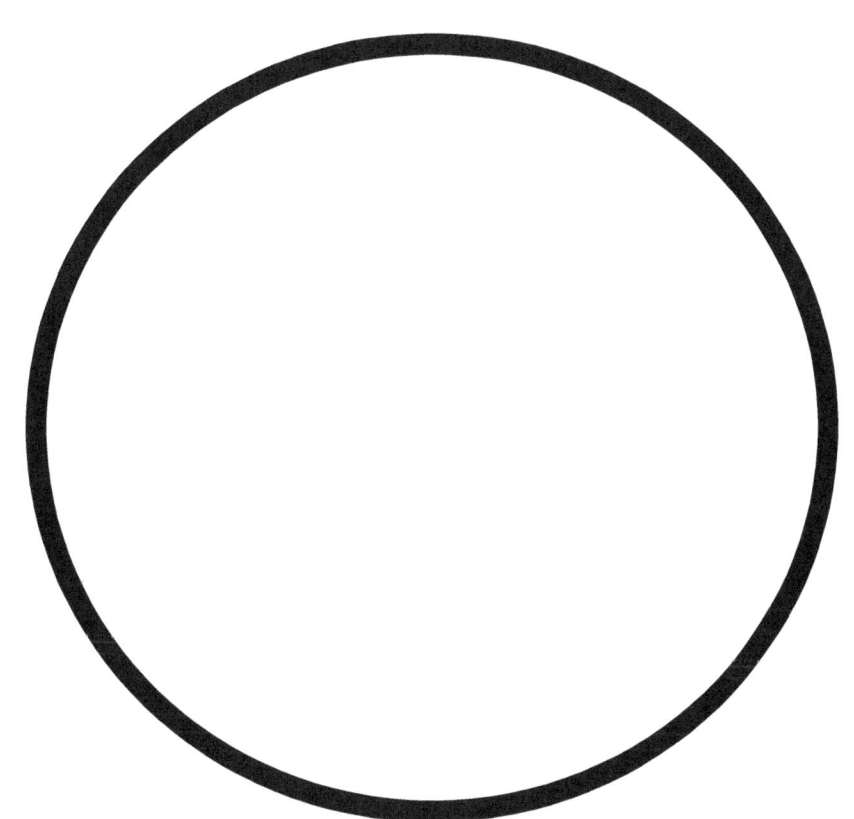

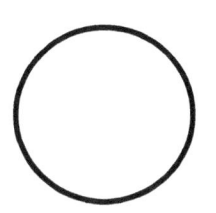

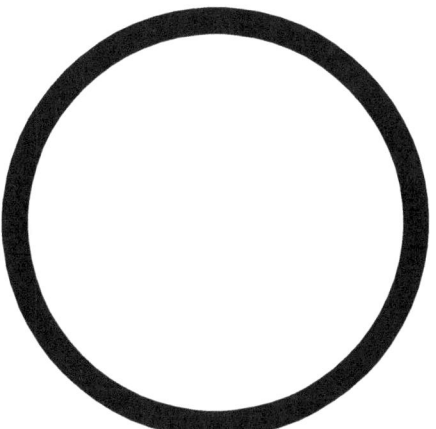

About the Author

Mallery Quetawki was born and raised in Zuni, New Mexico. In the Summer of 2009 she received her B.S. in Biology with a minor in Art studio from the University of New Mexico in Albuquerque.

As an artist, Mallery evokes the powerful history of her people through her art. Her style of work pays homage to her culture by portraying ancient symbols and designs throughout her work. An important goal of hers is to combine traditional and contemporary Native American art and make it work successfully as one. Her roots are traditional but with modern influences. She hones several signature styles and designs one of which is the storyteller owl pottery. In both her 3-D and 2-D works she also uses cross-hatching as a signature mark for her work. Other motifs widely seen in her products are butterflies, rosettes, and the rain bird.

Mallery is currently living and working as an artist. She is the mother of a son and daughter who inspire her everyday. She has been an active artist participant at the Indian Pueblo Cultural Center in Albuquerque, NM, both as an Artist Series instructor and an artist of a permanent display mural at the establishment. Other noted works include, "What Makes a Zuni?" also on permanent display at the Zuni IHS in Blackrock, NM. Her oil painting depicting the ties between the Grand Canyon and Zuni culture is part of a traveling collaboration called the Zuni Map Art Project hosted by A:shiwi A:wan Museum and Heritage Center. The map art is featured in the book entitled, A:shiwi A:wan Ulohnanne - The Zuni World by Jennifer McLerran & Jim Enote. She is the recent 2012 Easter Fellowship recepient from the Wheelwright Museum of the American Indian in Santa Fe, NM. The Fellowship will fund future coloring books as well as full-color children's story books written in the Zuni Language and English.

Other books by the author:

Zuni Pottery Designs to Color: 30 Modern Twists on Ancient Motifs
ISBN-13: 978-1467984447
2011

Examples of Mallery's work can be found at:
www.zuniartisan.webs.com